Raising Great *Girls*

HELP FOR MOMS
To Raise CONFIDENT, CAPABLE
Daughters
(perfection not required)

DARLENE BROCK

The Grit and Grace Project

Contents

Published in the U.S. by:

The Grit and Grace Project, LLC

P.O. Box 247, Estero, FL 33929

info@thegritandgraceproject.com

www.thegritandgraceproject.com

Author photo by Nick Adams, nickadamsphotography.com

Cover photo by Megan Schaap, meganschaapblog.com

Cover design by Damonza.com

Revised and updated from original book entitled Help Wanted: Moms Raising Daughters

Print ISBN 978-0-9993684-1-1

Ebook ISBN 978-0-9993684-0-4

Acknowledgements

When I would lie in the grass as an imaginative little girl with all my dreams for life, writing a book was not among them. So, when I began this venture, I even surprised myself. But this project is one that took on a life of its own, in no small part because of the two little female humans who gave me the title of "mom."

So, the first two people I must thank, are Loren and Chelsea. My daughters who thrilled, challenged, exhausted, loved and taught me through our shared life. It was because of them; I learned the need for grit and the depth of grace. They have now grown into confident and capable young women of whom I am magnificently proud. They continue to inspire me every day.

To my husband, my partner in everything life, who watched this mother swing from feelings of confidence to those of abject failure and back again. He comforted me when I cried, listened when I ranted and commended me when all was well. He believed in me in every venture I had undertaken, especially in motherhood, even when I doubted myself.

To the girls at The Grit and Grace Project, who keep me on my toes and more in tune with our ever-changing world. Rachel Graham, whose abundance of suggestions, feedback and insights made this book better. Clare Marlow, whose friendship, support, contributions and encouragement have meant more than she will ever know. Ashley Johnson, whose strength, love of the written word and excellence in the craft inspire me to be more purposeful in all that I do. Julie Graham, my This Grit and Grace Life co-host, who has taken on the task to teach me the important things in life, like Emoji. But she inspires me with her energy, resilience, and determination to move forward no matter what life throws her way.

To Pamela Ham, my dear and trusted friend who was willing to read my very first draft of this work. She promised to provide me with honesty and possessed the courage to tell me if I should give it up. Fortunately, she didn't.

To the girls at Media Collective, you possess the skills to move mountains, or at the very least get a bunch of people interested in what you are pitching. You ladies inspire other women to never back down, doing it all with sweetness and a smile.

As much as we women like to think it, we cannot accomplish all we want to do without the men. To the men who have helped build everything I do, I want to say thank you. Mark Adkison, I have watched as ideas have erupted out of your brain to complete impossible tasks. Your talent, determination, and passion have helped build our businesses for a very long time. To Mick Ross, our SEO guru who painstakingly creates the opportunity for the searchers in the land of technology to find us. To Justin Hall, the guy who makes This Grit and Grace Life Podcast not squeal, thump or blast out your ears when Julie and I get excited.

For those who make me look good. Nick Adams who has shot most of my photos. A man who is always willing to drag the softbox (which is spectacular lighting that I want to clamp on my Walmart cart as I shop) wherever we go bringing out my best. To Megan Schaap, who spent a day taking a million photos for the cover, so my need for a bunch of options could be met. To Merritt Mizesko my little real-life cover girl whose precociousness shows in every shot and her mom Kelli who gave me everything and more to make this book cover work.

You would think I would have started with God because the truth is without him I would not have completed this book. In fact, some days I might not have gotten out of bed. But it is his faithfulness through all my life, not just the years of raising my girls, that has kept me going, made me strong, yes given me both grit and grace. Anything within me that is wise, good or right has been born of his amazing grace.

Introduction

NO EXPERIENCE NECESSARY

| JOB DESCRIPTION |

One of the most rewarding and challenging jobs in the world, raising great girls. No experience necessary...?

HINDSIGHT: THE ABILITY to understand a situation or event only after it has happened. A word that becomes abundantly apparent in every area of life as you ponder the past. It is also something I possess a lot of today, especially when it comes to the subject of raising great girls. You see, I have two.

When my hindsight takes a moment to list the riches of my life, my daughters take the lion's share. Perfect and exempt from life's pitfalls, they are not, very much like their mother. But they are amazing, talented, funny, passionate, and kind. They are indeed great girls, or now I should say, young women.

Whether the girls who are in your life came through marriage, foster care, adoption, or by birth, a mother's hope and desire is to raise them to be great ones—girls who have the grit to get through life with perseverance, standing up for themselves, as well as others. Also possessing the grace, they need to live each day with kindness, compassion, and understanding. They will not be perfect, nor will they be problem free. They will be challenging, illogical, willful, and some days simply confusing. They will also be wonderful, delightful, a treasure, offering a relationship that will surpass most others in your life.

In the years I raised my two girls, I was working in the music industry full-time, often traveling, logging long days and late nights. My husband and I were building our businesses, so it never stopped. But I loved the career I chose. I had always been passionate about my job, accomplishing it to the best of my ability. If I made a mistake in the task at hand, it was usually fixable and didn't throw me. I just tackled what I needed to do to make it right.

But the moment I found myself unexpectedly pregnant with our first daughter, I panicked. The job of "mom" was one for which I felt utterly unprepared and convinced that any mistake I made would not only be unfixable but would be the ruination of this child entrusted to my care. This was not a job I felt qualified to undertake.

I can tell you these things in hindsight—I was not prepared, at least not in the way I thought I should be. What I did discover was already within me existed the strength and tenacity I needed to tackle this new job. The life I had lived and the challenges I had faced had prepared me. I just didn't know it yet.

Indeed, I would make mistakes. Sometimes they were quickly fixable; sometimes they initiated a season of education. But more often than not, they were an opportunity for me to ask for and receive grace. These would become great teaching moments, as we moms like to say, for both me and my girls.

As the panic subsided, taking a deep breath, I gave myself a lecture—if I could pull off every other new endeavor of my occupation, there had to be a way to do this one as well. I had seen other mothers do it.

I believed that to have the best chance of accomplishing any new vocation; you need to find ones who had already apparently succeeded at the task at hand. I quickly sought good mothers to learn from what they had done.

The Super Bowl of Mothering

What better place to look for the "best-of-all moms" than the mothers of United States Presidents? I figured these women had to be the "Super Bowl" of mothering. It was in their stories that I discovered surprising facts about these women and stumbled across some great role models who gave this new mom hope.

Sara Delano Roosevelt

You may not know that Franklin Delano Roosevelt was reared by Sara Delano Roosevelt in a New England family of wealth and aristocracy. Franklin was well traveled and educated in the best private schools, even receiving a law degree from Harvard. This family lived with virtually no financial want.

When young Franklin was ill in the Groton School Infirmary with scarlet fever, his mother returned from Europe to care for him. In those days, scarlet fever was highly contagious. All patients were in quarantine, and only healthcare workers were allowed in the room. Undaunted, this resourceful mother dragged a workman's ladder to the second-story window of her son's room. Each day Sara climbed that ladder and tapped on the window. When opened, she talked to and read to her son, caring for him in the only way she could.

The refinement, dignity, and wealth of this world-traveled woman couldn't compete with the nature of motherhood. She would not be kept off that ladder. She was there performing her job when her son needed her most.

Dorothy Gardner King

It was in the year 1913, under the cover of darkness, that Dorothy Gardner King boarded a taxi with her sixteen-day-old son in her arms. They were fleeing from an abusive husband and father. Dorothy had grown up in a prominent family and married into affluence. In those days, a woman simply didn't leave a husband of position, especially with a child in hand. A divorce required that each act of violence be publicly detailed and witnessed, bringing unwanted scrutiny upon prominent families. Dorothy courageously did just that. She rescued her child from a life of violence, filed for divorce, and left an abusive household behind.

Nearly three years later, Dorothy Gardner King married a common paint salesman who had only an eighth-grade education. A delightful, loving man, Jerry Ford became the instant father of a three-year-old son. He promptly gave his full name to this child, Gerald Rudolph Ford, raising the boy as his own. The reward of Dorothy's unselfish act of protection was seen in the life of the 38th President of the United States.

Martha Young Truman

America's 33rd President, Harry Truman was the child of a family of farmer reared on the rich soil of Kansas. It was important to Harry's mother, Martha Young Truman that she taught her children hard work as well as personal innovation and culture. This middle-class family worked the land together, awakening at 4:00 a.m. to complete the farm chores.

But Martha Truman made sure her son was not limited but armed with the tools and dreams to achieve his destiny. Living within the budget of a family farm, Martha scraped together the needed funds to purchase an expensive set of books entitled *Great Men and Famous Women* by Charles F. Horne. Harry's education consisted of twelve years at public school, graduating with a high school diploma; he never attended one day of college. These works, given to him by his mother, fueled the inspiration of this young farmer's son. Because Martha recognized Truman's voracious appetite for knowledge through the written word, this mother sacrificed to provide the education and inspiration he needed.

A Doable Job?

The more I read about these women, the more I liked them. They had figured out their mothering style and found their mothering prowess along the way, and that gave me hope. If these women in their varied roles, financial statuses, and unique personalities could raise a President, my job as mother appeared doable. These were truly "ordinary" women who performed mothering tasks extraordinarily well. Other than the times in which they lived, they weren't different than we mothers today. They didn't know what their sons would become; they merely set out to face the challenges before them and accomplish their motherhood profession well.

I, like you are today, was destined to rear two females in the fast-paced, challenging information age in which we live. They would be growing up with multiple conflicting definitions of who they should be as girls and then as women. These ideas would not only come from watching my actions and hearing my words, but they would also from television, social media, film, education, music, and even Barbie dolls.

Other women in our culture, from their platforms as entertainers, businesswomen, politicians, teachers, etc., would be determined to help me train my girls (whether I wanted them to or not). Fear struck one more time as I realized there were many things I didn't want my girls to be taught.

I discovered then, and I can confirm with great assurance now, that this motherhood thing is not merely one job. Mothers are not just "Mom." They fulfill a variety of positions and responsibilities. We are required to be Professor, Counselor, Financial Advisor, and Coach; we must brainstorm, create, figure out, simplify, organize, protect, and encourage. And like many of you, I had to do all of this while fulfilling another job outside the home.

This book contains what I learned about the jobs moms need to master, insights I gained, the advice from other women that helped me, as well as some realities about the life and culture we live in that will inform your perspective. It also includes a section for dads. After being asked by dads if I had advice for them, I just had to add what I consider the three most important jobs done best by the man in our daughter's life. And to accommodate most men's reading style, I made it short and to the point!

As hindsight has shown me, I can assure you that there will be both success and failure. But I'm living proof to tell you this—Mom, your goal can be accomplished, and your hope can be realized! You won't raise perfect daughters, but you will raise great girls who will make a difference in the world in which they live. You will be proud of them, admiring many of their traits, in awe of their abilities, and encouraged by their passions and compassion.

So even if you feel unprepared, you can take this on, and Mom, you will do it well—the job of raising great girls.

-1-

COACH

Teach player techniques, rules, strategies, and tactics. Condition athlete for activities, strength, and endurance. Instruct player in sportsmanship, cooperation, work ethic, and responsibility. Monitor conduct of player and respond to injuries.

COACHING? YOU'RE SAYING. *What does that have to do with rearing daughters?* Everything. This is truly the first position a mother has to accept: becoming the Coach. If you're not an athlete, not to worry. I'm not, either. Playing sports wasn't and isn't my thing. As my girls were growing up, I had many other interests, including art and music.

But this job doesn't have a thing to do with athletic ability. You can be what was called in our home "a girlie girl" and still get this one right.

Immediately following the manual-labor tasks of motherhood, coaching begins. At the end of the early days, you know the blur when you believe sleep will never again be part of your life. Every few hours you feed, change diapers, burp, bathe, change diapers, feed, burp, pick up, rock, feed, burp, clean up, change diapers, bathe, and rock again…all the while begging God to give you both that much-needed rest. It's when the sleep finally returns, and these manual-labor tasks become automatic, you become the Coach. I can tell you with the clarity of hindsight that the effective performance of this position will, without a doubt, determine the success of every other job for the next eighteen years.

A Coach is the leader, the authority, the person responsible for the accomplishments of the players.

A Coach has to draw on experience and be confident in creating the plays—also a must for mothering girls.

A Coach sets the team rules and consequences for inappropriate conduct; so, does a mother.

A Coach responds to injuries; well, I can tell you firsthand there's a boatload of those in mothering daughters.

A Coach motivates and inspires—a crucial duty of mothers.

And a Coach is well aware that each player is an independent decision-maker. If the players have a good coach who leads them well, their good decisions become much easier and their bad decisions less desirable.

A Coach is the leader, the authority, the person responsible for the accomplishments of the players.

Friend—or Mom?

For quite some time there has been a groundswell, parents seeking acceptance and friendship from their children, especially when they are teens. I have observed those who are willing to buy their children everything they want, say yes to every ask, to accomplish their primary objective: to be their child's best friend. In theory, this sounds like a good plan. Who doesn't want their child to like them? to share private thoughts as a friend would? to hang out? to have deep, meaningful conversations and friendly fun?

But there's an unintended byproduct to this desire: to maintain a position of friendship, one must abdicate a position of authority. Friends are generally not instructional. Friendship does not discipline, set rules, protect, give insight, and seldom challenges incorrect acts. Parenting does. Friends don't usually inspire and motivate you to become more in life. Parents do. By desiring to be a member of the friendship club these parents are missing a significant reality. A child will have many friends, but as parents, we're it.

Whether you are a birth parent, a foster parent, an adoptive parent, or a stepparent, the privileged role you play in your daughter's life is exclusive. You are not part of the team; parents are the Coach. You are singularly the most influential person in your daughter's life.

I can't stress enough how important this job is. No one can replace your role and make an impact on your girl the way you can. This relationship is vital. Without it, the effects on your daughter will be immense and will last forever. Does this bring fear? Indeed, it should. But don't let that thought paralyze you. Motherhood is a manageable task if you stay the course. And just wait—at times it'll even be inspiring when you, as the Coach, see your daughter make that winning play.

You are singularly the most influential person in your daughter's life.

For all of you mothers, like myself, who experienced days (or months or years) of relational panic with your daughters, I have a wonderful piece of "after the fact" knowledge to give you hope. There will be times you wonder if your daughter will ever become your friend if you're an effective Coach. You'll watch that daughter storm off toward her room and desperately wonder, *"Will she hate me forever? Am I always going to be the one who just doesn't understand?"*

Real-life experience with both my daughters taught me that neither of those fears is real. If you're committed to being a great mom and you maintain the position of Coach that your daughter needs (whether she wants to admit it or not), you will become her friend. And the relationship formed will be a much deeper, more meaningful one than she'll have with her peers. The kind of relationship that transcends time, distance, and life obstacles. A relationship that runs so deep your heart will thrill with what you and your daughter mean to each other.

The mother who performs her duties from a fearful, pacifying place, always trying to be her daughter's friend, will never have the privilege of experiencing this profound relationship because the daughter will not develop a healthy respect for her mother. But the mother who holds firm to the position of Coach? She'll be the one to experience lifelong benefits.

Experience Is a Great Teacher

It takes strength, determination, and courage to maintain this leadership role—a strength that comes from confidence in your abilities, talents, and knowledge you have garnered in life. This is the time when you, the mother, must evaluate who *you* are, aside from your roles, and believe you are capable of undertaking whatever you decide to pursue.

Most coaches were, at one time, players. How do they begin their jobs as coaches, then? They call upon the experience they gained by simply performing the tasks on the field, in the court, wherever their sport led them. It is no different for mothers. Begin by drawing upon your experience. You were once a girl, dealing with bad hair days, the challenge of multiplication tables, boyfriend struggles, and the vicious putdowns of mean girls (that is, unless *you* were the mean girl. But I'm quite sure you've left that behind). Life has taught you what you need to know to relate to what your daughter is experiencing right now and along the way. And you can use that knowledge to both of your benefits even when you get the "you don't understand, Mom. That was a million years ago" line.

I must put a caveat into this discussion, for the moms who are dealing with circumstances they personally never encountered. You may be the mom to an adoptive, step, or foster child whose life circumstances before they became part of your family, surpass those that most have experienced. If that is true, expand your sources and resources. The fundamental position of coach is still yours to assume and maintain, but some of the play-calls may be entirely different.

Coaches also watch a lot of tapes. You know, the ones that show how the other team makes their plays, what their mistakes are, and areas where they are weak. In addition to watching other players Coaches closely watch how their team is performing. This is relevant to you, Mom. You or someone you know has made a multitude of life decisions and actions that led to specific consequences:

› Driving too fast can wreck a car.

› Run out in the street; you get hit.

› Put a kernel of corn in your nose; it can get stuck.

› The way to get pregnant is to have sex.

› Touch a hot stove; you get burned.

You've seen these consequences; perhaps you've lived them yourself. They aren't rocket science. So, add all of these "truth and consequences" statements to your information base and set the rules, determine the plays.

Use your strengths

Think about what you have accomplished in your previous or current "career." What classes in school did you excel? In what jobs have you performed the best? Which of your talents accomplished success in your past? Are you a good organizer? Do you inspire others? Are you creative, logical, or mathematical? The duties you perform, as a mother will draw upon the same abilities as those you have already used.

Take time now to write your list of strengths and then ponder them. They'll be just what you need for this motherhood job, as well as using the information you have collected while living your life.

My List of Strengths

> _____

> _____

> _____

> _____

> _____

> _____

> _____

> _____

> _____

No coaches are identical in their abilities, and neither are mothers. Your unique mothering style—your strengths, talents, and the way you live your life will be a perfect match for your girl. So instead of trying to be like everyone else, why not be exactly who your daughter needs? You! It doesn't matter if she entered your life through childbirth, adoption, or marriage, *you are it—the one and only!* You can, and you will do your job well.

But that doesn't mean there won't be days when you'll be thinking; *I don't have a clue what to do. I'm out of control, my daughter's out of control, and I just want to stop this world and get off.* Like fighters going to their respective corners, you'll need to send your daughter to her room, and you'll need to go to yours, so you can both calm down and process rationally. At such times, when you know you're over your head, take a step back. Remind yourself that this job can and will be accomplished by you. Then leave your corner with a clear mind and a confident heart and begin again.

Instead of trying to be like everyone else, why not be exactly who your daughter needs? You!

As difficult and daunting as this work can seem, I can assure you it's amazingly simple. Simple rules, simple plays, simple consequences—as they say in team sports, "back to the fundamentals." In our multitude of theories, books, and philosophies regarding motherhood, it's easy to lose track of the simple. I believe the mothers before us understood this principle far better than we do today. That's why we can learn so much from them.

Gutsy Grandma Bunger

I was six years old, playing in the living room of my great-grandmother's home, one of my favorite places in the entire world to be. That's because Grandma Bunger was a special lady. Four-foot-eleven, mother of twelve, she had some of the best costume jewelry, hats, and gloves ever seen by a little girl. On each visit, she would let us cousins raid her closet and parade down the stairs, tripping over too-big shoes, hats falling into our eyes, and our arms so heavily bejeweled we could hardly hold them up.

We were the cousins, fourth generation. We landed on our grandmother's doorstep like an army invading the Promised Land. Having twelve children of her own, Grandma Bunger had a plethora of grandchildren, which were our parents, and even more great-grandchildren. I couldn't count how many of us there were. All I knew then was we had fun.

We spent our days together dressing in her clothes, going through her junk drawers, (which held delightful treasures) and eating our meals in every corner of the house. The parents and grandparents would talk, argue, laugh, and cry together. The smells from the kitchen would be sweet.

This day was no different than most, the family was busy visiting, mostly talking over one another as they often did, and laughter was abundant. Suddenly a massive commotion arose in the kitchen. I heard the voices of Grandma, Aunt Juanita, and Uncle Jack, and it didn't sound good.

Then the clamor headed my direction—from the kitchen, through the dining room, into the living room, and right out the front door. Grandma was chasing Uncle Jack, a six-foot, more than two-hundred-pound man, through the house and out the front door, hitting him with her broom. You see, he had come home drunk, and when drunk, he could get mean. He hit Aunt Juanita, and Grandma would not have any of this.

So as a young girl, I watched as Uncle Jack ran for his life. He was no match for this lady. Grandma, less than half his size, meant business and we all knew it. She knew the fundamentals. To her, life was simple. This conduct was unacceptable, something that she would not tolerate, no matter how big the challenge.

Grandma Bunger was my hero.

But lest you think she was perfect, so you can't relate to her, let me tell you a little more about this grand lady. Ethel Anna Berry was born July 1, 1881, in a small town in Indiana. She didn't live a flawless life; she had a fair amount of heartache. In May 1899 my, not-married grandmother bore a son. I can only imagine the plight of an eighteen-year-old, single and pregnant before the turn of the twentieth century.

Two years later she married my great-grandfather, a man who never accepted her out-of-wedlock child since he was not the father. Together they had another eleven children. Sadly, she outlived several of her children: two died as infants, one in a war, and another from cancer.

Grandma Bunger indeed had a tough life with an abundance of trials and struggles. The woman I knew was kind and loving, often smiling, as she lived as the pillar of a very diverse family. Working hard through the week, sewing the family clothes, gardening and cooking, performing household duties on machines in ways we can't begin to understand with today's technology. She had a full-time job with these duties in addition to raising her children. Sunday morning found her with gloves and hat on, dressed in her Sunday best for the weekly church service.

Grandma Bunger was strong: she knew exactly who she was, what she believed, how she wanted to live, and what she wanted for her family. Although she dealt with life's limitations and the consequences of choices—as we all do—she predetermined which goals she wanted to achieve and stuck with the basics. Embodying grace, perhaps because she lived under its umbrella. She knew the fundamentals, backward and forward. We as mothers can pursue the same thing—with the same success!

Acting as Coach

A Coach assembles a team, seeking members with abilities to help win a championship. They believe in those players, know their potential, and will take whatever action is necessary to ensure that players maintain the conduct required to reach the goal. A mother is no different, except for one area: we don't draft our daughters to join the team. (Some days you might wish there had been a daughter draft and perhaps you could have chosen the less-argumentative version, but it just doesn't work that way.)

Bench 'em!

The one thing we must do is take action to maintain conduct. We have to be willing to bench them. When necessary, we have no choice but to discipline. This knowledge I gained from real-life exhausting experience.

I'm a coffee drinker, the kind who has to have two cups of incredibly strong coffee in the morning to carry on an even somewhat intelligent conversation. Before that dose of caffeine, I stare and stumble to the kitchen, grumbling the entire way. My family knows to stay clear, and my husband has my first cup of coffee made and waiting on the counter for the moment I arrive (self-preservation at its best).

When Loren, my first child, turned two, she was unaware and uncaring of this inadequacy of her mother. She was out of bed every morning and ready to hit the ground running. But with this willful child, the first act was almost daily one of defiance. I contend that those who believe humans are inherently good have never had a willful two-year-old. There is no stronger evidence of sin nature in humanity than the two-year-old who is defiant for no other reason than they want to be.

Our mornings would begin much too early with repeated calls of "Mommy" emanating from her bedroom. I would finally appear at the door to her room and stumble in to get her out of bed. The constant source of noise in our home, Loren chattered from the moment she awakened. I would hug her, kiss her, and carry her to the living room, setting her in front of the television to watch *Sesame Street*. Then off I'd go for that first life-saving cup of coffee.

From the time I left her watching Big Bird, to the moment I returned with coffee in hand was never more than two minutes. The kitchen was only a few feet away, and all I had to do was pour (thanks again to my husband). However, it still amazes me that, in that brief amount of time, I couldn't complete even that simple task without my daughter challenging some level of authority. And the repertoire of her willful acts was huge.

Even though armed with the knowledge that the dog's tail was not to be pulled, I would find her chasing him with a vengeance, leaping upon him with tail firmly in hand. Or she would tiptoe from her seated position to the bookshelf on the other side of the room. From the kitchen, I would hear book after book tossed onto the floor. Sometimes my return from the kitchen would not find her in the den but the bathroom, dunking her toys in the toilet with glee. It was when I encountered this willful child that I gritted my teeth, steeled my will, and set to work.

You see, I was the Coach, and this was my job. When my daughter defied the rules, I had to enforce them. I must say, these weren't some of my most valiant life moments; they were born of necessity. I was not brave. In fact, some days I helplessly looked around the room for anyone else willing to fill this role. When I would plead "At least let me drink my first cup of coffee," Loren would stare me straight in the eye and run headlong to fulfill her mission. That two-year-old was smart. She was challenging my authority at my absolute weakest moment, and she knew it.

There were days in that battle period of my job that I was ready to throw in the towel. Every time I thought, *I'm too tired today. This one instance won't kill either of us, so I'll just let it go and ignore her,* I'd remind myself, *this same will is going to turn sixteen. She'll date, drive a car, and leave for college. If I don't hold to the rules now, what will she try to do then?*

Envisioning this defiance in a child driving a car and missing curfew struck terror in this mother's bones. I knew I needed to be in charge while she was still shorter than me. To succeed in the task of motherhood, I couldn't shrink from the challenge, no matter how difficult it turned out to be.

But know this, Mom. If you didn't enforce the rules when your daughter was two, or she wasn't in your life at that age, you still can. And you still should. At six or sixteen, it's never too late. Will it be harder? Certainly. Your daughter will also have more verbal responses than a two-year-old would, but the defiance is the same. There are days you'll have to bench your daughter.

How do you do that? The ways to bench change with temperament and age (hers not yours), the circumstances that have shaped your girl's life, and of course, the offense. Most often the best penalty is the one that matters to them the most. It may be a favorite toy, time on the computer or the phone, a time-out. I do believe spanking may be appropriate, determined by the recurring nature of the offense, and temperament of the child. But whatever punishment you feel appropriate benching them is imperative.

Why discipline with something your daughter loves? One of my daughters hated time-outs. Not being able to be in the middle of life made her miserable. My other daughter had a dreamland that resided in her mind; she could visit it while sitting still in time-out and be happy as a lark. So, time-out never worked for that child. That's why it's a must to pick your daughter's discipline, appropriately.

Get used to "Monday Morning Quarterbacks"

Has there ever been a coach for any team who is not criticized, challenged, or second-guessed? There's an easy answer to that question: nope, nada, absolutely not ever. Even if you are not a follower of sports yourself, you've heard the grumbling from the group in your family room. This is true in the role of mother as well. Your mother, mother-in-law, friends, society, schools, churches, and even your very own daughter can become "Monday Morning Quarterbacks."

They will feel the need to tell you what you did wrong. So, you didn't always call the right play, didn't bench the player when you should have, or you benched the player when you shouldn't have. Well, so what? I've done them all. Take advice from the sources you trust and leave the rest at the door. Got enough to deal with without having to listen to them. I can tell you this with absolute certainty; it doesn't take a perfect coach to be a great coach.

These duties might sound ominous to you. Let me tell you; they're not the most enjoyable tasks. But put them in perspective. When your thirteen-year-old daughter marches up the steps proclaiming, "I'm so mad at you!" your heart probably isn't warmed. Most likely, you're mad at her too and hopefully trying hard not to show it. Then an hour later she returns to rummage for food in the kitchen. (Get used to it: teenagers are always hungry.) She plops down next to you on the couch and proceeds to make a complete cookie, cracker or organic trail mix mess. All the while she's chattering away, and it hits you: *She still likes me.*

It doesn't take a perfect coach to be a great coach.

Then there are days you feel someone must have gotten this one wrong. Who decided you were capable of being the mother of a daughter, especially to this one who has her unique personality that can make every self-assured bone in your body crumble? Or mom to the girl whose challenges you did not even know before she left another family to become a part of yours.

When all of these self-doubts hit, let me assure you: You were made to be the perfect mother for your daughter. The pairing of the two of you is no accident. You are equipped with the talents, abilities, and gifts not only to do this job but to do it well. Your daughter was given to you and you to your girl. You and your girl are not perfect people, but you are a perfect match.

There will also be the days that you will realize your inspiration and motivation has paid off. Your daughter has made a good play! The multiplication tables are learned, the mean girl is brushed off, and recovery from heartbreak is achieved.

Trust that on the great days, as well as the hard days; you will find the right words, the right actions, and the right responses to coach your girl successfully. Concentrate on doing this job first, and the rest of the jobs become a little easier.

-2-

CREATIVE COUNSELOR

| JOB DESCRIPTION |

Cultivate a positive climate that will encourage the child's uniqueness, gifts, and creativity. Establish a relationship with the child based on the counselor's understanding of counselor's and child's creativity and purpose. Create activities that ensure the development of all talents and gifts innately within the child.

ACH SUMMER, WHILE I was growing up in Indiana, my mother would help me tackle a new project. One year we made a dollhouse out of a cardboard box. Another time we redecorated my bedroom—from pink frills to trendy paisley wallpaper on, of all places, my ceiling. These summers taught me at a young age, how amazing it is to be creative and embrace originality.

But one particular year remains special in my memories—the summer I was learning to sew. Armed with a 1960s Singer Sewing machine, fabric, snaps, thread, straight pins, and scissors I began that year's project. My mother was determined to teach me to sew, and what better way to learn but on clothes for my Barbie dolls? I wanted the most stylish anyone had ever seen, and my mother was going to help me.

So, on a Saturday we made a trip to the local fabric store and discovered preprinted fabric, the kind where the skirt and top shape were printed onto the muslin fabric, and all you had to do was cut and sew. We picked out and purchased the only selection they had.

Once back at home I began my quest for creativity and, from my mother's point of view, my initiation into sewing.

Diligently cutting out the shapes with my mother by my side helping me, I labored over the fabric. No more of the Mattel manufactured outfits for me. I was forging a new path. My dolls were going to have distinct clothes uniquely made for them. I carefully cut and pinned each piece. Placing my foot on the sewing pedal, I often ran it far too fast as I got used to the rhythm. (I'm sure my mother held her breath as I barely missed stitching my finger.) I sewed every tiny item on the one-yard piece of fabric. I'm sure there were no more than two or three outfits, but it became my mission to finish them all.

After days of cutting, pinning, and sewing, my creations were complete. I was delighted. I had brand-new clothes that *I* had made for my Barbie dolls. None of the neighbor girls had the same ones I did. I was delighted with my accomplishment.

That is, at least at first. You see, the problem with preprinted fabric was that it was available to everyone. The only thing any little girl had to do was walk into the fabric store, purchase the same length of fabric we did, and their dolls' outfits would look identical to mine. It didn't take long for my excitement about my creations to diminish. Every Barbie doll would look no different than my own—the very thing I wanted to change.

It became imperative to find something I could do again to set my Barbie dolls apart; which became my mother's and my next pursuit. At the same fabric store, we made a discovery: you could buy patterns to make clothes with the fabric of your own choice...even using the fabric, you already had at home. I carefully selected the appropriate patterns for the clothing I wanted to create.

Arriving home with the sack in hand, I was anxious to begin. Laying the patterns on the small pieces of cloth left over from dresses my mother had made for me, I pinned them carefully. I was successful in this endeavor, only sticking myself once or twice. A Barbie doll skirt was my first independent creation. It was rather simple to cut the semicircle pattern, sew it, and put a snap on it, but I felt I had made a great accomplishment. Next was the matching top. This was a little more difficult. The pattern was more intricate, and the cutting had to be more exact. With help from my mother, I accomplished this task too.

This cutting and sewing went on the entire summer. Taking scraps of material left from my mother's sewing projects, I made clothes for my dolls. In fact, I created an entire wardrobe! New dresses, pants, formals, skirts, and tops for my dolls matched my clothes—all with patterns from the fabric store. I was really on a roll. Never satisfied, I decided it was time to make my original designs.

Now the real fun began.

Out with the patterns, I was going to sew freestyle. I took the scissors and cut what I thought would be an appropriate length for a formal dress. Sewing it together on each side, with the ribbon on the neck and fake fur around the hem, I concocted one of the most original Barbie formals ever seen…even if it didn't hang quite right, the seams were a bit off, and the ribbon crooked. Then, to top it off, my mother had enough scraps of fake fur that I could make a coat for my doll to match. A bulky, furry thing that probably could have fit two Ken dolls standing side by side. But I was delighted. This was one fine outfit! Barbie was ready to go out on the town.

That formal Barbie attire turned out to be only the beginning of my original designs. Of all the things I made that summer, my favorites were the ones made of my dreams—not using any preexisting pattern, but only what I wanted my creations to be. They were dresses and formals, skirts and accessories that were uniquely mine. They had buttons, rhinestones, and sequins in the strangest places on the most unusual clothes. To me, my Barbie had never looked finer.

Astonished by Originality

As I was reading, taking the few minutes I try to set aside before I begin my day, I was abruptly struck by a verse in the Bible that nearly flew off the page. Since my attention span as an adult is still equivalent to a three-year-old's, I occasionally have to be jostled to heed what I need to hear. The words were ones I'd heard before, yet suddenly they seemed fresh and alive:

Do not conform any longer to the pattern of this world,
but be transformed by the renewing of your mind.
Then you will be able to test and approve what God's
will is—his good, pleasing and perfect will.

—Romans 12:2

As I often do with Scripture, I immediately thought, *What in the world does that mean?* Nonconformity to a pattern, transformation, and then you will find God's will—not only that but his *perfect* will?

In my faith, I base all assumptions upon the fact that I believe in a divine creator. A God who is supreme, original, and enormously smarter than I am. He would have to be to have made this world. Everything he created was indeed freehand—no pattern—and he apparently has the same expectations of us.

In a quest to discover what is meant by originality, the antithesis of patterns, the most appropriate place to begin is in creation. Have you ever gone to a zoo or an aquarium? In every creature, you see there is originality galore! Stay even closer to home and sit on the grass in your backyard or a nearby park. I'm not talking about sitting in a chair but *in the grass,* where you are in the middle of the activity. Observe the flowers, bugs, bees, butterflies, rabbits, lizards, blades, leaves, tree branches, bark, sky, clouds, and the wind's effect. Take in the sights, sounds, and smells. Follow the movement and detail around you, the simplicity of the sky, the complexity of the flower petal, and the energy of the bugs and animals.

If you pay attention, you'll be astonished that the color green is a million different shades and hues. There is no end to the creativity right outside your door. Beautiful, original and harmonious, every corner of creation offers amazement. Yet, try to define the Designer. Talk about not following a pattern; God set the standard for originality and uniqueness. His innovation through the creation process is reflected in the marvelous world around us, as well as in the intriguing individuals he created. There is not one item in creation that is identical to another.

Take noses, for example. The next time you're in a meeting with a group of people, sneak a peek at each person's nose. (You can get by with this kind of examination since the nose is so near their eyes; they'll just think you have good eye contact!) After your survey, you'll be surprised by how different they all are—fat, narrow, long, short, with a bump in the middle, at the end, or no bump at all. Talk about creativity, and that's just a nose!

The Patterns We Conform To

In this creative nature is one of our most important jobs as a mother—that of Creative Counselor. But to understand and effectively counsel on originality or creativity, we have to first understand the *counter* characteristic—sameness or patterns.

The purpose of a pattern is to duplicate something. *Webster's* dictionary defines it as "a form or model proposed for imitation." An item of clothing, a repeated design on wallpaper, a mold for metal piece reproduction, the flight path of an airplane—these are all examples of patterns. To follow a pattern, we continue on the same route again and again—a path that has already been created and traversed. When I consider the Scripture that states we are not to conform to a pattern, I believe we, as mothers, are charged not to reproduce what we see but to be original. And we are tasked to rear originals as well.

A requirement to train our daughters in the avoidance of unoriginality means realizing and pondering the two patterns we find ourselves conforming.

The normal route cultural offers

The first pattern is created by the world we live in and by the paths of people around us. We should never follow others' lives and actions just because they do so, and it seems the normal cultural route. I still remember my mom saying, "If your friends jumped off a bridge, would you?" As much as I hated that phrase as a teenager, I've said the same thing to my daughters when they were teenagers. The temptation to repeat some things your mother told you is simply irresistible, isn't it? After all, there is fun in watching the rolling eyeballs.

The first pattern of this world is one that encourages duplication and discourages individuality while at the same time pretending independence. This pattern is designed to destroy your daughter's uniqueness. It will end in the degradation of their self-esteem and derail them from their life purpose.

It's easy for us to look at the world of music, film, television, the internet, social media, the sexual revolution, and even the clothing industry as having a detrimental effect on our children. But if we're truly honest, we must also look at soccer teams, the current women's movement, ballet class, education, poverty, the American church, and the moors of the middle class. Some of the most effective influences over and diversions to the well-being of our girls are subtle. All wrought while we try to fulfill all the cultural expectations we place upon ourselves. So, Mom, it's time for you to take the bull by the horns. Examine every one of these influences. Dissect them to determine how to control their result. Look around and figure out what unhealthy influences are hitting your daughters. Then decide how best to handle the information from this time forward.

A very real problem with the pattern set before us from our culture is its hidden sameness. This is teaching young girls a value system—and it's available in nearly every medium (television, movies, magazines, books, etc.)—that's destructive to the self-worth and confidence of our gender.

My elder daughter was thirteen when she announced she was getting a tattoo.

Here's what I mean. Every mother has at one time, or another heard the all-too-familiar phrases that go something like this: "But Jennifer's mom said she could go" or, "It's what all of the girls at school wear." Then here's one of my personal favorites: "All of my friends get to do it...you just don't trust me." Mom, it will take all of your originality and creativity to respond, but you must. Why would you follow a course just because "everybody's doing it, or thinking it, or saying it"?

My elder daughter was thirteen when she announced she was getting a tattoo. She was the child who was terrified of needles and cried each time we headed to a doctor. I knew she'd never face a needle voluntarily no matter how much she wanted to make me think this was imperative to her life goals. So, I happily went along with it. I told her getting a tattoo was an important decision, because it was permanent. I said I'd be more than happy to go with her and look at what kind of image she might want. We could even go to the library first and see if we could find books on tattoo designs. Indeed, this tattoo would be with her for life, so it should be quite lovely.

Loren was disappointed that I didn't take the bait for a fight. At that particular stage of thirteen, she was only interested in irritating me. To show me she was all grown up and independent, she had determined to do something she thought I might not like. But when I didn't react negatively, it was astounding how quickly that conversation was forgotten. Not another word was said about a tattoo ever again.

Now if you're reading this and you have a tattoo, let me be quick to say I'm not making a judgment on tattoos. I've seen some incredibly beautiful ones. Talk about creativity—talented artists have fashioned some of these designs, and they are indeed a work of art. But thirteen years of age was not the time in life to decide on something that permanent. A decision like that probably should be made when you're at least thirty. Don't we all change our minds on almost everything after thirty? It's better to wait until you're at least out of high school to do something that's not easily changed.

But that day when my daughter announced her tattoo, I had a choice. I could respond with the traditional, "Oh no, you're not, young lady. You absolutely will *not* get a tattoo!" or I could face the confrontation with an original approach that gave me a much better chance at success with this willful thirteen-year-old.

And guess what? On that day, success was mine.

You see, originality and creativity do work. And it gets your daughter's attention, too.

Then there's my younger daughter, Chelsea. She had pink hair in elementary school. Yes, I realize that's a bit different from the norm, and some mothers would be extremely uncomfortable with hair that color, but for Chelsea, it was self-expression. We only streaked the length of a few strands or the hair ends, but she loved her pink hair. And each time we varied how we put in the color. So, when she asked me about it the first time, I said we could do that; we'd make it a mother-daughter project. *How odd,* I thought. *My mom taught me to sew, and I'm coloring my daughter's hair pink to spend time with her.*

My daughter Chelsea had pink hair in elementary school.

Off Chelsea and I went to the artsy downtown store that sold weird temporary hair color and purchased one jar labeled Bright Punky Pink. After dinner, we spent the rest of the evening accomplishing her creation. How we dyed her hair was her choice. It was her style and design, and she was very particular in the execution. Putting on the color-safe gloves and wrapping my daughter completely in old towels, I placed pink hair color in two-foot lengths of hair on each side of her sweet face.

The next day my eight-year-old attended elementary school with pink streaks. She was delighted with the look. I have no idea what the other mothers thought of either Chelsea or me, and I didn't care to know. What others thought didn't matter. My focus was on what's most important: doing whatever it takes to build a strong mother-daughter relationship. With my girls, I always wanted to allow for originality and creativity.

Many things were priorities to Loren and Chelsea that didn't matter to me. They were not life-changing ideas. Early on, I had committed to give my best to my daughters by focusing on the issues that were important in the long-term, not the ones with short-term effects. They could have pink hair if their hearts were compassionate. Unusual and unique clothes didn't scare me if they maintained modesty. Multiple-piercings would be in the family budget if they concentrated on their school work and worked to achieve life success.

The art of creative counseling requires a mom to focus on the imperative issues to help ensure life success.

Your crusade as a mom is for the hearts and souls of your daughters. That's why, short of an indecent wardrobe, clothing doesn't matter, hair color doesn't matter, and even tattoos and piercings don't matter. Those are all short-term things. So often we find ourselves doing battle over the small issues and alienating our daughters before we can even get to what matters for their futures—like their self-esteem, their values, and their faith. Don't spend time fighting the unimportant battles. If you do, you'll lose the real war.

Instead, be creative, allow uniqueness, and watch your daughter flourish into a genuinely great girl.

Great expectations

The second pattern we fall into is one of expectations—those conscious and subconscious ones we've developed long before our daughters entered our lives. Every mother expects her daughter to follow the course she (the mother) knows. But perhaps you are an accountant, and God gives you an artistic daughter who has never understood coloring within any lines. Or you garden, producing and eating only organic produce, then daily slip into your Birkenstocks, and your daughter wants to become an entertainment lawyer. Imagine a woman who is a politician, always in the limelight, and her daughter wanting to be a stay-at-home mom in the carpool lane.

That's where a mother's counseling in personal creativity must get *really* creative. It must not only ensure that your daughter follows a path of growth in character and principles, but that she also pursues *her own* place in our human race. The one uniquely designed for *her*…not the path *you* choose for her or one of others' expectations.

The girl entrusted you with is not a clone of you, and she's not her sister or her cousin. She should also not be conformed to the image of what others—your mother, mother-in-law, neighbor, friend—think she should be. This is not to say there might not be invaluable advice from each of those people. But each premise, yours or theirs, must be tempered with the nature of your daughter. Are your expectations based on what's best for your girl—or do you hold to them because it's what you know, what you've heard, and where your comfort lies?

To do the job of motherhood well, we need to be confident about who we are—even when we don't know how to handle a situation. We need to know what our worth is, what we believe, and how we want to live. If we understand these important issues, it will be easier to guide our daughters to do the same. To perform effectively the duties of a Creative Counselor, we are required to set aside our comfort and do our best to help our daughters follow their course…all the while maintaining their individuality.

Living as a true original

Nellie Cashman is a great example. Though not much has been written about her, I find her series of adventures fascinating. Born in Queenstown, Ireland, she and her older sister, Frances, immigrated to America in 1851, when Nellie was sixteen years of age. Arriving at Boston Harbor, they stayed one year, then boarded a transcontinental train for San Francisco, California.

Nellie signed on as a single woman at the age of twenty-three to a mining troupe as the cook and set out for the Cassier Districts in the mountains of Juneau, Alaska. Nellie was a lone, petite, attractive woman, but she held her own. Even in the mining camp, the men treated her with dignity and respect. She worked alongside them, cooking and mining, and suffered the same hardship, success, and disappointments they did.

After a year in the mines, she left Alaska in the fall to venture into the larger city of Victoria, British Columbia. Upon arrival, she received word that a fierce winter storm had trapped the men she left behind. They had exhausted the major portion of their food, and they were seriously ill from scurvy and couldn't make their way out.

Nellie purchased potatoes and vegetables, the nutrient-rich foods needed to treat the disease, hired six men to join her expedition, then turned right around and headed back to the mountains. Traversing the ongoing winter storm, Nellie and her hired companions made it back to camp in time to save the lives of her prospecting friends. The mining community's hearts were won, and Nellie became known as "The Angel of Cassair."

Nellie's endeavors included a restaurant in Tombstone, mining in Nevada, and another business in Montana.

In Tombstone, Nellie was well-known for her passion and compassion. Early one morning, she, along with a few men she'd hired, demolished gallows built to hang five murderers. This wasn't done because they were innocent, but because the city was charging admission to the execution. She thought everyone "should die with dignity." After her morning demolition project, she went to the jail and spoke with each man, giving them the opportunity for one last confession. It was their souls that interested her.

Her sister, Frances, was by now widowed and had been left with five children. When Frances was injured from a fall in 1880, Nellie immediately moved to live with her in San Francisco and help take care of the children. Three years later, upon her sister's death, Nellie took it upon herself to become parent and caretaker. Never having married, she moved the children to her home in Tombstone and into her life.

Once back in Tombstone, Nellie again rescued another human. When the price of silver decreased at the Grand Central Mining Company, angry employees were overheard planning the kidnapping and lynching of the mine superintendent.

Hearing of their scheme, Nellie paid a visit to the superintendent's home. After a brief stay, she leisurely drove into town down the main road, then abruptly turned into the railroad station. Jumping out from under a blanket in the back of her buggy was Superintendent Gage. He leaped onto the platform, jumped into the train, and left the city with his life.

After the children were raised, Nellie moved back to Alaska to the territory she loved. This Alaskan legend, known as the first female prospector in this challenging land, lived in a cabin, traveling twelve miles by snowshoes to get her mail. At age seventy she was still mushing (running behind a dog sled) and set a record that year as she mushed her dog sled 750 miles in seventeen days and became champion musher of the world.

I tell you this story because Nellie lived a life I'm pretty sure her mother would never have planned for her. Looking into her sweet daughter's eyes Nellie's mother may have envisioned Nellie playing the piano and raising socialite children while entertaining with her mayor husband.

Like many other little girls of her era, she could have chosen a domestic life far easier and much less physically challenging. But that was neither Nellie's course nor her character. Hardships and adventures were a mainstay for her as she led the tough life of a pioneer.

And because she did so, lives were changed. Men about to hang were allowed to face their death with dignity. Miners lived to prospect again. Her valiant rescue of the mine superintendent not only saved his life but stopped those who were angry from committing an act they would regret the rest of their lives. Her sisters' children were reared in love and confidence. And Nellie was friend and caretaker to so many others.

Nellie followed a pattern that would have made sense to very few, yet countless lives of those around her were made better by her unexpected choices.

I have absolutely no information on the mother of Nellie Cashman, but I feel rather confident that she had to have reared her daughters to follow their own course. It is what we must do as well. If we unwittingly force a mold upon our daughter because of what we or culture expects her to be, others will miss being the beneficiaries of things *only your daughter* may be capable of doing. But if your daughter is encouraged to fulfill her unique place in this world, she will indeed leave a powerful legacy in the lives around her.

Then you, my friend, will have been a very successful Creative Counselor.

TIME MANAGER

| JOB DESCRIPTION |

Create the principles and systems individuals use to make conscious decisions about the activities that occupy their time. Responsible for developing strategies directing time and motion studies to promote efficient and appropriate utilization of personnel and facilities.

I T WAS TUESDAY. My elder daughter sat in the front passenger seat of the car, changing the station on the radio at least once every minute and thirty-three seconds. You see, she was incapable of listening to any song in its entirety. First verse, chorus, second verse, and she moved on. My younger and her friend were in the back seat talking continuously—about what, I had no idea. I was driving, late to their gymnastics class and on my cell phone with a calendar in my lap, changing a business meeting I would not make.

I had picked up one child from middle school and the other two from elementary. I was driving back by the middle school because it was the route to the gymnastics class. Logic would have it that I should have gone to the elementary school first, then middle, but of course the school dismissal times would not cooperate with this line of reasoning.

Knowing I was late, yet not paying an enormous amount of attention because I was placing a call, I failed to realize I was back in the school zone. You know—the one where the speed limit drops from 40 mph to 15 mph when suddenly I heard the abrupt siren. Looking in my rearview mirror, I saw the flashing lights of a police car directly behind me. My heart sunk to the bottom of my stomach, I pulled over and stopped. The officer walked toward my driver's door, peered in the car, and asked me if I was aware I was driving 40 in a 15. What could I say? I had three children with me and was speeding in a school zone. This zone was designed solely for the protection of children, including those in my car.

Sheepishly I said, "Sorry, I should have known better. I was late for an appointment, and I wasn't paying attention," etc., etc. I had that sick feeling you get when you know you are in the wrong, and you desperately wish for a do-over. My husband would be so frustrated because this is the second ticket I had gotten for speeding in less than one year (and admittedly those were the times I got caught).

I had that sick feeling you get when you know, you are in the wrong, and you desperately wish for a do-over.

There go the insurance rates, I thought. I begged, pleaded, and told the officer my entire story, yet I still got the ticket. He felt sorry for me but said there were a lot of speeders in the school zone and the police were on a weeklong crackdown, ticketing everyone they pulled over. He was nice, doing his job, and unquestionably in the right. What else could I have done but meekly take my ticket and say okay?

The police officer did compliment us on all having our seatbelts on. But when I told my husband that to try to soften the blow, it didn't work.

He was not convinced the seatbelt issue was enough. Perhaps not speeding directly in front of the school would have been a better option. Yet, I was always late.

I was late to pick up my girls, late to dance class, late to business meetings, late to gymnastics, late to dinner. You name it; we were late. We had so much to do. My husband and I were building our businesses, my girls were growing up, and I wanted to be in their lives. I wanted them to have every opportunity, learn all of life's valuable lessons, be brilliant in all endeavors, be involved in everything available to them—and all before they were finished with the lemonade stand on the street.

We mothers enroll our daughters in soccer, ballet, modern dance, T-ball, basketball, art, music, and gymnastics. I have always envisioned a cartoon of a child wearing a tutu, with a helmet on their head, a number on their shirt, basketball, bat, paint supplies, and musical instrument cradled in their hands while dancing on tiptoe. Who is this child anyway? Are we expecting any girl to possess all of those gifts and excel in them by age eight? At the same time, they have to attend school…and get straight A's, of course.

In hindsight, I can emphatically say that we mothers are officially nuts. The idea that our children should be involved in every activity available is unequivocally wrong. We have created a family circus that exhausts our daughters emotionally, physically, and mentally. And that's not even taking into account *our* state of mind.

The busier we are achieving all of the "programs," the more we miss out on precious time where we could be experiencing life together with our families. Achievement by volume is not achievement—it is distraction.

When you involve yourself in every activity, you miss the important ones. Instead of my daughters observing me breaking the law in a constant state of overdoing, I wonder how much better they would have fared if I had taken the time to sit with them and look at the stars? But we were all too weary from our run-around days.

So, what's the solution?

Stepping out of the Family Circus Ring

No one wants to be involved in the family circus of exhaustion. But to get out, we have to choose to step out. We must become effective Time Managers. We must slow down, evaluate the schedule objectively, then decide when we want to get into that car and drive. Allow yourself to ponder—does that extra trip you're making this afternoon matter to your daughter's life, success, and well-being in the long run—not to mention your own?

Identify natural talents

The way to manage time well is to understand your daughter first. Every child is talented, but every child does not possess every talent. It's seldom in life that we find the athlete who is also a musician, or the mathematician who is also a painter. It would be unlikely for an engineer to be a politician or a dancer to be happy sitting in an office. Happiness and fulfillment will be found in what we are good at and have a natural inclination toward. Instead of enrolling our children in everything available we serve them better by finding out what their natural talents are before we begin.

To understand the appropriate commitments for your daughter, begin your research by exposing her to as many options as you can. Note that I didn't say *sign her up* for the classes or events. Instead, take her to the soccer games to watch, the concerts and plays to observe, the art museum to look at the paintings. Watch to see when your daughter's eyes light up, listen to her evaluations of the event, and ask if she wants to return to that place. Whether she's excited or not will be telling. Is she watching raptly, anxious to experience more? Or has she wandered off to find something else to do, wiggled nonstop until intermissions, or drawn on whatever scraps of paper you have in your purse until it's time to go home?

Observation is a key to choosing activities to fill your family time. Does she enjoy tackling her brothers or cousins? When she goes outside to play, is she headed for the basketball goal or the sidewalk with the sidewalk chalk? Maybe she creates art projects out of her food, sees colors at a young age as not merely blue and red but as navy, teal, burgundy, or red-orange. Perhaps she tells delightful, imaginative stories.

---

*Every child is talented, but every child
does not possess every talent*

Don't limit your daughter to activities you consider "for her gender." This is not about gender confusion. Instead, it recognizes that the breadth of talents and abilities exist in both boys and girls. There are the girls who want a train set or building blocks; if so, perhaps you have a future architect. Some daughters collect bugs, frogs, and pull worms into two halves to see which direction each part slithers. When music plays, does she sing into her hairbrush, hit the pans in the kitchen rhythmically, or dance through the living room? Maybe she acts out scenes from her life—a dramatic actress before the age of five.

These may not be scientific assessments, but they are Time Manager indicators. A part of your job is to look carefully *before* you sign up. To check out the signs before you cross the metaphorical commitment street— the signs that read Warning: Exhaustion Ahead, Undue Pressure for All, or Leap Only When Massively Prepared. If you perform the job of gathering the data on each child, you'll choose to sign your daughter up for one class, two classes, or no classes at all.

When mother guilt strikes

I have to warn you, though. There's something unique to *mothers* who are Time Managers. Most people who fulfill these duties of responsible decisions for efficient time management sleep well at night. They don't think about what they *didn't* do. We moms, on the other hand, have boatloads of "mother guilt." You know exactly what this is because there's not a mother on the planet who has not experienced it. It's the emotion that hits when your daughter wants to invite a friend over to play on Saturday, and her friend's mother informs you there's no opening in her daughter's calendar.

The conversation between mothers goes something like this after school, when you're both in the pickup line at the curb:

You: "Olivia would love for Charlotte to play with her Saturday. They've become such good friends at school."

Other mother: "Oh, sorry she can't play on Saturday. Charlotte has soccer games. They start so early that Friday night is out as well. What team does Olivia play on?"

You (limply): "She doesn't."

Other mother (raising an eyebrow as if reconsidering your motherhood status): "Well, we've been involved with soccer teams since Charlotte was five. We think she could play pro one day. But she loves basketball as well. Last year her team won state finals, you know. Oh dear, I must get back in my car because I need to be the first in line. Charlotte has to be at dance in twenty minutes, as well as working on her art project tonight. I can't forget to pack her violin for tomorrow's lesson, either. Is Olivia going to take swimming classes, go to the Y camp, or enroll in the community art center this summer? Perhaps the girls could see each other then."

You stutter a reply: "No." Then creatively you add, "Our family will be busy spending our summer helping to design the new space shuttle that will launch from the Kennedy Space Center in the fall. You may know they retired the old one."

As you crawl back to your car, you know you must be a failure as a mom, for running beneath the conversation you hear, "If you were a good mom, Olivia would not be available Saturday, either."

Fear hits the middle of your stomach. What if you failed at your motherhood profession because you chose to keep Olivia home instead of joining the T-ball team? What if your daughter is a complete failure in life because you have denied her an abundance of activities?

Mother guilt weighs like a brick wall as you sink further into your car seat. You want to be a good mother; you don't want to miss any opportunity for your daughter. What if you alter her success by choosing not to sign up?

Putting Busyness in Perspective

It may come as a surprise to most mothers, but historically women achieved all kinds of success before we ever invented events for our youth. They became doctors, lawyers, business owners, artists, musicians, and scientists, leading successful, fulfilling lives. Again, one of the most valuable reinforcements of this philosophy is the women of history themselves.

Molly Pitcher

You may have heard of this incredible woman before. She gave water to soldiers on the battlefield during the Revolutionary War for America's independence. She was a tobacco-chewing, hard-talking, tough mama. When the soldiers were losing the battle because of thirst, not only did she bring them pitchers of water, but at one point she took over the loading of the cannon for her husband and shot it herself. He had collapsed from exhaustion; she hadn't.

I doubt that Molly Pitcher had to play T-ball to learn to be a team player.

Betsy Ross

This "flag lady" didn't just sit in her living room, sewing the first United States flag on her lap. She ran her own business, which was hired to make this symbol of newfound freedom. General Washington met with her, holding a rough, hand-drawn rendition of his concept. Knowing her business as she did, she changed the proportion of the stars, rearranging General Washington's drawing. Then, together, she and the General made a new sketch that was used to tailor the first American flag.

Do you think Betsy Ross's mother signed her up for a year of art lessons to accomplish this success? No, the only thing Betsy was probably taught as a little girl was how to sew. The rest came from her creativity, originality, and her business skills.

The price of overachievement

This phenomenon of unrealistic overachievement has been perpetuated in the last fifty years. Sadly, during this same time, the rate of suicide, depression, anorexia, bulimia, and clinical exhaustion have climbed astronomically. The win-at-all-costs attitude we've adopted has placed our children on the altar of self-destruction. If the philosophy holds true that busy is better, then our busy children should feel better about themselves...they don't. They believe they aren't smart enough, talented enough, pretty enough, or anything enough to feel confident in their self-worth.

What's the answer? We need to return to what's simple. To a philosophy that self-esteem is gained by who you are, not what you accomplish. Time management is not merely a time or energy issue; it's an issue of self-esteem and character.

Something so often missed when keeping our daughters so busy is that they don't have time to appreciate the world around them. Lost is the beauty when you don't spend the time observing it. The simplicity of a flower's structure and purity of its design is only seen when you examine its clarity. If your daughter has never studied the night sky and marveled in awe at its wonder, how can she understand the majesty of God and his care for her?

Psalm 8:3-4 says:
When I consider your heavens, the work of your
fingers, the moon, and the stars, which you have
set in place, what is man that you are mindful
of him, the son of man that you care for him?

In the midst of our constant state of busyness, do we take time to see the stars? Or do we miss out on the beauty and the wonder? The magnificence of creation is far grander than any activity or event.

Time Manager mothers of today are faced with one challenge in our technology entrenched society that mothers in times past were not: It's

Saturday morning, and you have left your daughter at home sitting on the sofa in the family room checking her social media accounts and texting her friends as you run errands. Grocery store shopping, car's oil change, and dropped the dog at the vet, all tasks complete, you arrive back at the house… only to realize that your daughter has not moved. She is in the same clothes, in front of the same screen, repeating the movements you observed before you left. Sure, you gave her the list of chores that needed to be accomplished before you returned. But while you were gone, she has been lost in the abyss of her current social realm for hours, not realizing her morning is gone.

That daughter of yours is texting her fingers to stubs posting every moment of her existence. Not a good idea on any level. But it is a mainstay in her life nonetheless.

Then, walking toward her room early evening, carrying on a conversation (one-sided), you approach her doorway to find this precious girl staring blindly at her computer or her tablet, grunting responses with no realization that you are in her universe desirous to communicate. It is these moments you realize between all the devices she has at her disposal your daughter has succumbed to a newfound malady: the "I am an electronic zombie losing all track of time or purposeful existence" disease.

In the age of brilliant new inventions—and they truly are—the discoveries that inform, entertain, communicate, and enlighten, we have to guard against them taking over. Your girl's cell phone, video game, computer, and any innovation that enters your home can transform from being a part of your daughter's life to consuming your daughter's life. When technology leaves the realm of a useful tool with a noble purpose and becomes the center of her universe, then it's time to set the timer. You may have to limit the smart-phone usage, turn off the tablet, or take away the computer for a period. Just don't be afraid to take whatever steps needed to keep technology in its rightful place.

When technology leaves the realm of a useful tool with a noble purpose and becomes the center of her universe, then it's time to set the timer.

So, Time Manager Mom, manage this time consumption as you do with every other item your daughter is involved. You will instruct, monitor, and control. Set the standard, set the limits, and be in charge of the time lost in the world of technology. Do not be afraid to allow her to experience the benefits of these useful innovations, just limit their influence. If you succeed at this one, they can glean the meaningful, fun, and educational elements of this great technological age without falling into its consuming and controlling snare.

In our distractions, wherever they come from, we may also miss the people in our lives. There was a time in history when children were taught relationships and cooperation by being part of a family or community unit, not as part of some other kind of team that changes every few months or every year. And absolutely not through social media groups.

I know many of us don't live in the same town as the rest of our family. But Manager Mom, make time for your children to create relationships in the community you live in with people of other generations. The role once played by grandparents is lost in our mobile, fragmented society. The wisdom of ages is not shared with our girls because they are not in our daughter's lives. But learning from this generation, as well as learning to care for them, wields profound personal results in every next-generation daughter.

My father-in-law stayed with us for five months while recovering from difficult hip surgery. He couldn't walk without a walker for quite some time, and when he did, it was not very far. As a result, he was confined mainly to his room and was very dependent on us while his body healed. Caring for anyone 24/7 is exhausting, no matter how much he or she means to you. There were times my husband and I needed to take a short break.

During one of those instances, we left our daughter Chelsea, seventeen years old at the time, in charge of her grandfather for the evening. When we arrived back home, he was fed (grilled cheese), his medication had been given, his personal needs had been attended to, and even his room was straightened. Chelsea did it all on her own, missing nothing and spending time just talking with him as well!

I couldn't have been more proud. It was one of those "I must be doing okay as a mom" moments, because my daughter had grasped what was important, and she had been responsible and reliable when left in charge. When I told her that I was proud of her, she simply shrugged, said, "No big deal," and headed back to her room. A minute later she was on the phone talking with a friend—with music blaring.

Somehow in the midst of those teenage, self-absorbed years, my daughter had gained the understanding that time spent caring for someone you love is indeed well spent. My mother side could only sigh and say of my daughter "all is well."

So, mom, become that effective Time Manager. Learn that you manage time; it doesn't manage you. Control the time-consuming distractions in our technological world. Discover who your daughter is, what talents she possesses, and enroll her in *only* the things appropriate to her natural gifts and interests. Ignore that mom in the carpool line. She'll soon be hospitalized from exhaustion, and the girls can play together then. Make time with your daughter to experience the beauty of the world around you. Finally, help your daughter know and love the people in her life, those of all generations. This, above all, will show your success as a great Time Manager.

-4-

MEDIA DIRECTOR

| JOB DESCRIPTION |

Oversee the media department with the responsibility of managing the client's media buying and planning needs. Carefully calculate media placement through research and analytical models to determine what is best for the client based on the product/service and the client's goals.

SEVERAL YEARS AGO, I was sitting in a hotel room in West Hollywood, California. That week I was there to work as well as visit Loren, my elder daughter, who lived in Los Angeles to pursue a career in the entertainment industry, which she has since achieved. That this is her dream didn't come as a surprise to us; she's been on this track since she was in elementary school. Loren is passionate, committed, driven, ambitious, and determined to make her mark in this business.

That in itself is enough to make a mother lose sleep. If you have never visited the City of Angels, there is no way to describe what a crazy place this can be. I have traveled throughout the United States of America and visited almost every state in the union as well as an enormous number of cities in all of those states. I've been to Chicago, New York City, Houston, Boston, Washington, DC, Dallas, Atlanta, as well as every other metropolitan community we have in this country. There is no place like LA. The capital of film and television sets its own path and makes its own rules. Some things produced here are great, creative, entertaining, and brilliant. But others? Well, they're not. Some who work in this business are amazing, others, they are not.

When your daughter is young, you tell her happily that there is *nothing* she cannot do. "Follow your dreams, honey!" you say. You know she has been created for a very distinct place in life, and she shouldn't let anything stop her. "The world is at your fingertips," you tell her, "so dare to dream!" Those are the days when you use every predictable and trite quote to give her determination.

Then your daughter grows up and has the audacity to take you up on your speech. You find yourself on an airplane with your baby girl, who is no longer a baby. Flying thousands of miles from home, you deposit her into a place she has chosen to call home. Your task is to help her settle in, give her a huge hug, then load yourself into the rental car and head back to LAX to take the red-eye home. After all, you'll be mumbling incoherently to yourself and tears will be streaming the whole eight-hour plane ride, so why not lose sleep too and get a bargain flight?

But the kicker comes when you're sitting in the airplane, surrounded by the snores of other passengers.

"Follow your dreams, honey!" you say.
Then your daughter grows up
and has the audacity to
take you up on your speech.

You are thinking '*What was I doing when I said, "Follow your dreams?"*
Was I completely out of my mind?' Amazing! The one time your daughter

listens and trusts what you say brings a result that you hadn't thoroughly thought out. I mean, thousands of miles from home in this foreign land we call Los Angeles? Couldn't she be just a little closer to home, and in a "safer" location?

But I did mean what I said back then. I wanted her to do exactly that: Follow her dreams.

Now Loren is, and I am glad. Not that she has lived in an often angry and sometimes mean world. Not that she has faced the exhausting challenge of moving from location to location, living six months at a time, working 12-hour days to master her industry; but that she was willing to take the risk to follow that dream. This business and especially the city of Los Angeles can be tiring—at least to me. So many people, so little grass, and so much concrete.

Not to mention that the interstate highways running through LA mirror the exact personality of the industry she has chosen—six lanes of bumper-to-bumper traffic heading one direction well exceeding the speed limit until everyone hits their brakes. If they're lucky, the cars come to a simultaneous stop. When they get tied up in traffic, the car owners honk and yell curious phrases at one another.

In the same way, there's not a lot of grace, mercy, and kindness displayed by the collective front of the entertainment industry. The claim of tolerance is often belied by their reaction when faced with those who don't think as they do. Many are only accepting of those who are like-minded and adhere to their standards. The stand of protection of the weak and equality among their ranks has recently been in question. The curtain pulled back by the allegations of misconduct from some of the most powerful belie the protection of the most vulnerable. They are often creatively and culturally different from the majority of America.

An Assembly of Folks

But now that Loren's been in the entertainment industry for several years, she has met some delightful, loving, and kind people—individuals she cares about very much. Even ones that can disagree with her on most ideological conversations, she has grown to love well because she has shared life. Watching her has reminded me that all we consider a "collective mass" is truly comprised of individuals. We have to remember that in every industry, the powerful can take advantage of those who serve under them. Wealth, self-importance and success lead many to act in ways that not only harms their business but hurts those around them. But I believe we often react most strongly to this industry because their product helps shape the minds of our children and the culture in which we live.

We have to remember that no matter what title this group holds, it is not a headless blob but an assembly of folks from every walk of life, from every state in the union.

As parents, we often spend a lot of time making a ruckus over the entity called *entertainment* and its agenda but forget that the entertainment business is made up of people. Individuals with mothers, fathers, sons, and daughters live in this community and work within this culture. It is not a collective army of anger even if some days, the outspoken among them are angry. This business is comprised of real people with hopes, dreams, heartaches, births, deaths, with all human needs and wants. Understanding this concept is a crucial aspect of confidently fulfilling the position of Media Director.

Effecting change

It is our responsibility to neither dismiss nor become afraid of the entertainment world. It only has the power we give it to affect us. It can change and shape us, or we can change and shape it. The choice is ours. What I do know is it must not be ignored.

The remarkable part of entertainment is not its effect on us but our effect on it. As I learned through my business life, as well as the life of my daughter, this medium is a collection of humans with a dream to perform, create, and produce. We should not be angry at this group of individuals by what is produced any more than we are at auto-manufacturing workers when our car breaks down or the cell-phone salesman when we can't get a signal. We just need to address the strengths and weaknesses of this industry to effect change. To do that, a Media Director gathers research and understanding of who comprises the industry prior to making "buys" for our client—in this case, our daughters.

So, step back and take a different view. Instead of looking at the world of entertainment as if it is the threatening "blob" from the 1958 horror film, understand that you are in control. In fact, each of us has all of the control we choose to accept. But to make this task manageable, you must first understand the people involved in media and how we affect them. To begin, they come in two pretty simple forms, the performers, and the behind-the-scenes folk.

Each of us has all of the control
we choose to accept.

Performers

Performers are drawn to their profession out of need—to deliver art, to be liked and accepted. The talents that make them want to be on the performance platform are couched and driven by that need. They want to please, delight, entertain, and gain the attention of an audience. And they need to accomplish this for their satisfaction as well as ensuring that they remain a viable part of an industry that brings the world the arts (not to mention bringing home a paycheck). When an audience doesn't embrace their craft, a performer is tremendously unfulfilled. A theater without an audience or a song without a listener is a sad creation.

The success of performers is defined in several ways.

There is the immediate success of a job appreciated by an audience, reviewers speaking accolades in print or on television about an artist's performance.

There are the awards presented by peers. At times this can serve as the catalyst to continue a path of "creativity" even when the sales or audience is absent. Being encouraged by your peers through accolades or reviews, while comforting at the moment, is a temporary reward for a need that remains.

The single most visible determinant of success is the sale of records or music downloads, concert tickets, television ratings, streaming numbers or box office revenue. By this barometer, the companies that fund the projects will determine their continued involvement with the artist. If a performer doesn't make money for a company, eventually they find themselves no longer with a job. A megastar can last through a few disappointing box offices but, without ticket sales to back up their pay scale, they will lose favor. Their passion is not fulfilled, nor is their opportunity still available.

Behind the scenes

As an observer, as well as a participant in the business side of entertainment, I understand that the people behind the scenes drive much of the content. They often have an agenda and purpose in what they produce, again sometimes noble, other times not. But the fact remains that if they want to continue working, they have to succeed financially. No matter what the agenda is, without financial success they cannot—and I repeat cannot—continue in their business.

Who creates the media's financial success? We do. It's pretty simple. It may take a couple of bad movies, low music sales or TV ratings, but the outcome is inevitable. If their projects don't make money, they are out of work.

That means we, the consumers, are the most significant influencers of entertainment. It is up to you to determine who will win the audience and what kind of productions you will support. You can choose for them not to influence you and your daughter. I'm not saying boycott, just *choose*. Be the one who directs what your daughter hears and sees, and when she sees it. Be informed and aware of the content of movies, for example, before you allow your daughter to see the latest release with a friend.

This job of Media Director is one of the most demanding. A significant amount of time is required to succeed at this position. You must spend the energy and time to research what entertainment is offering your family. When was the last time you watched YouTube, researched movie titles or television shows, or listened to music targeted to your daughter? Do you know the iTunes list of Top Song and Album downloads, the current

Billboard Top 100, or the Top Ten Box Office Movies? What are the highest viewed YouTube videos? Are you aware of the "only famous for acting stupid" phenomenon? Of what determines the definition of G, PG, PG13, and R-rated movies? What language is allowed, what sexual content is contained in these productions?

It's so easy for time to fly by…and suddenly you find yourself in a world that is your daughter's but one you seem to miss entirely.

It's All About Oversight

The majority of mothers begin their lives as "mom" gazing into the precious face of an infant. Looking back, the memories are sweet, aren't they? It was a special day, the day that you and your daughter met for the first time.

Whether your infant girl was yours by birth or adoption, the day you brought your child home was the one you'd dreamed about, pondered, feared, and anxiously looked forward to. It was merely a few short days before this, most likely, that you saw her beautiful face, held her hand, and changed a diaper for the first time. This precious bundle was your girl—she was real! Before she was born, she seemed like a dream, a kick, indigestion, discomfort, a foot in your ribcage, or a concept and hope in the midst of a stream of adoption paperwork.

Perhaps a few months into the pregnancy you went to the doctor with expectations, then saw her on the ultrasound. Well, what you saw was a blur—a foot, a head, or some other body part. But as the technician explained what you were looking at, your eyes marveled at seeing your precious daughter on film for the very first time. You knew then she was *your baby*, even if, to others, she looked like just a fuzzy blob!

For those of you who adopted, you saw an image of a child…and fell in love. The reams of paperwork and months of preparation fell away as you stared transfixed at the tiny photo from another state or from overseas. Or perhaps you were allowed to see the child right after birth.

You couldn't wait to welcome that child into your arms.

Those first few days at home

Finally, the day arrived—no fanfare, no parades, only tears, and agony until you first saw her treasured face. Then one look at that sweet and precious baby and you knew: you would do *anything* to care for this little one.

You learned her cry, her yawn, her squiggly face that you swore was a smile but was probably indigestion. You fed her, changed her diaper, and had the gracious help of the hospital, birth center or adoption staff to make sure you weren't messing up too badly. They were there to help you do most things right. So being a mom didn't seem that difficult—at least not in that environment.

But then came the time to take her home. It was the day to begin your life together—your real life. You dressed her in the carefully chosen clothes picked out for her trip home. The car seat was already in the car waiting to be filled—after all, you set it up a month ago in anticipation of the happy event. You bundled her for cold even though it was 80 degrees outside, fearing some germ would touch her new life. With your daughter in your arms, you leave the hospital through the automatic door often accompanied by some precious volunteer who tells you what a beautiful girl yours is. Although you realize that volunteer has seen a million babies, ugly ones at that, you know they are right this time. Your daughter *is* beautiful.

The car seat is triple checked to make sure the belt is sufficiently tight. You strap your treasure in for the first time and check all of the buckles over thoroughly before you get into the car for the drive home. Opening the front door, you climb into the passenger's seat to turn around and look at your daughter, making sure she is ready for the journey.

In a panic, you realize she is facing the back of the car, can't see you, she may be frightened, and you just need to get back there with her. So, you roll out of the front passenger door and make your first mother move by sitting in the back next to the car seat, so that she won't be scared. You don't even notice that she sleeps the whole way and would have been fine.

The drive home is uneventful, her first car ride safe and secure. She has arrived home healthy, with no accident or disaster on the way, and is only whimpering a little. The motion of the car seems to fascinate her, then lull her to sleep. Pulling in your driveway, you wait until coming to a complete stop, as the car is placed in park you begin unbuckling her from her car seat.

What a memorable moment when you walk through the door with her for the first time. She is your baby girl, and she is home!

Now the work begins. You change diapers, rock her to sleep, and feed her every few hours' day or night. To say you are tired is a vast understatement. Pondering when you had your last night of real sleep, you stare straight ahead. *Months,* you decide. Now it looks as if you may never sleep again. You begin to panic.

And that precious little girl of yours can cry. We're not talking delicate whimpers; these are earth-shattering wails, and they don't end. Even the neighbors are covering their ears.

It looks as if you will never sleep
again you begin to panic

It's midnight. She's screaming again, and it seems nothing will make her stop and go to sleep. So here you are one more night, buckling that baby in the car seat, counting on the fact that car motion still lulls her to sleep. This time you quadruple check the restraints because you're so tired you aren't sure you did it right. At 1:00 a.m. you find yourself driving around the block to get some peace. At 1:15 you have pulled back into the garage and are snoring in the front seat of the car, treasuring whatever rest you can get, while your daughter is sleeping in the car seat. You dare not move, or those vital sleeping minutes may be interrupted. That car is the best bed you've slept in for what seems like an eternity.

But it's not only the lack of sleep. It's also the feeding.

How many times can a baby be hungry? Heavens, it seems you are continuously preparing formula or nursing; the process is never-ending. No breaks for you to eat a nice dinner yourself. You dream of the day your daughter can sit up in her high chair, put the food into her own mouth, and chew. Just the simple stuff—macaroni and cheese, spaghetti, chicken pieces, vegetables…anything that would be served at the family table.

When will she be ready? You wonder. First, it's the mushy vegetables, the mushy fruits, then the mushy meats. I think whoever invented mushy meat must have been having a majorly "off" day—such disgusting stuff. But real food—the bits of fruit, vegetable, and bread that can come from meals prepared for the rest of the family—doesn't arrive for months. You're exhausted by the process of trying to get the little bits into your baby.

Mmm…maybe she can handle the "unmushy" version of food sooner than other babies, you think. *She seems pretty smart. She might be quicker at everything. Let's give that toothless child a piece of steak.*

It seems like it would be a great relief to fast-forward through some of those first steps, doesn't it? After all, if you start her earlier on table food, you can rest a bit more. So really, why not?

Fast-forwarded kids in a media-heavy world

Wrong! Nothing your child grows into being able to handle, can or should be fast-forwarded. That includes food, crossing the street, tying her shoes, brushing her teeth, or learning algebra. Life is to be experienced by your daughter when she is ready and has been taught and is prepared to handle it. Even if you're tired and it looks like so much work to make sure she isn't exposed to something before she is ready, you have to protect her. Even when you are weary, you must remember that other people have an agenda contrary to yours. If you are tired and don't want the battle, you still cannot give in.

There is no place truer of this concept than the world of entertainment. There is some fare in the entertainment world that no one is old enough to consume and shouldn't be experienced. But there is a lot of the entertainment world that has merit, value, and even pure distraction from the mundane side of life. Music, movies, the internet, and television have a time and a place in your daughter's life. Knowing what and when that is, becomes crucial for a mother who is rearing girls in our media-heavy world.

I'm not sure where we got the idea that it's okay to let our children be exposed to the world of entertainment without guidance and instruction. They need our oversight. As in all things, this requires balance. We must protect but not overprotect. We cannot shelter them from everything entertainment offers. If we attempt to shield all exposures, they will be sent off to college ill-prepared to handle what is thrust upon them from this medium, because media is at its height of influence in these years. Yet as our daughters grow, we allow the world of entertainment into their lives well before they are ready to handle it.

My father was a great teacher. He wasn't an educator by profession, but an effective instructor to his impetuous daughter, me. I know I drove my daddy crazy because I was always following roads that made no sense. But while I was paving my path, my father was determined to teach me his values. Whether I ended up embracing them or not he made sure I understood what they were.

We were not allowed to use any profanity in our home. He loved language and words of all types, but I never heard him say a curse word or tell an off-color joke. In fact, he would make us learn words on a regular basis; we would pronounce new words for him, spell them, define them, and pronounce them again for him. We did this repeatedly until he seemed satisfied that we had gained one more vocabulary word in our repertoire. I believe it was his love of language that made the ones used even more important to him. But I digress. The point is that the words he would not allow us to say we were entirely aware of.

While I was paving my path, my father
was determined to teach me his values.

When I was fourteen, traveling in our family car, I convinced my daddy to turn on the radio station I wanted to hear. On came the song "Sunshine," by Jonathan Edwards. It was a fun little ditty, one that I loved to sing along. While I was happily singing the lyrics in the back seat, my father, sitting up front, was listening. Most of the time a girl would be delighted that her father was listening to her musical ability. But this time he was listening not only to me but the *lyrics* as well.

Suddenly the volume knob was turned down. Startled, I looked up, quit singing, and realized that Daddy was in control. He merely said, "Sweetie, keep singing." Oh, brother, I was in trouble. I wanted to do anything but continue the next line. But my father wasn't a man to give up when he was making a point. He said again, "Keep singing." So, I had to complete the next line in the chorus, "But he can't even run his own life, I'll be damned if he'll run mine."

No one had to say another word. I was nailed! I had been caught using a word unacceptable to my father, and even if it was just a song lyric, that wasn't allowed. It may seem like a minor offense, the word itself was, but I'll never forget the lesson of that moment. Heart racing, palms sweating, I knew the lyrics in the music I was listening to was not okay with my daddy.

Why did he do that? you ask. He wanted to make sure I didn't accept something he didn't approve of just because my culture did. He wanted me to think through my choices and actions. I doubt that he expected me to align with the values he was teaching me completely, but I do believe he understood as a parent it was his job to set an unambiguous standard. Now that's a smart parent. For me, it was a lesson well learned.

While your daughter is gaining knowledge of the medium, it is your job, as Media Director, to guide her. If you know your rules, understand the world of entertainment and the culture it is creating for your daughter's consumption, you will be able to do so wisely as my dad did. You should *never* accept from entertainment a lifestyle diametrically opposed to the one you are creating for your daughter.

Are film ratings enough?

We gain much of our information on films from the rating systems. They are designed to tell us what age is appropriate for our children to see various movies. But the irony is that no one knows who determines the standards for these ratings. The members of this board are anonymous. Never having met a single one of those people, why should you use their standards as yours?

Have you ever once in your life made a decision suggested to you by a group of people you didn't know? If you didn't know who they are, where they live, or what their life criteria is, would you trust them with a key decision in your life?

The rating system is no different. It may indeed be correct, but the only way to know is to investigate the content yourself and make your determination of the age-appropriate material that will be delivered to your daughter.

Also, *you* are the only one who truly knows your particular daughter. Each child is influenced differently in life. Sensitivities in your first child will not be the same with any other children you may have down the road. All children are individually responsive to input and should be treated that way when determining what appropriate fare is.

But let me be quick to say that it would be equally wrong to shelter your daughter from the world around her completely. Just as you fed her the appropriate food at the appropriate time, there is an exposure to information that is vitally important under your instruction.

If you completely protect your daughters from anything in the world outside your home, they will be unprepared to handle it when they go it alone. And they *will* go it alone. So, they must be allowed to experience entertainment through your eyes.

You may say they should never see an R-rated movie, and at a young age, this is infinitely true. But teens can be potentially impacted positively by films such as *Schindler's List, Saving Private Ryan, The King's Speech, American Sniper* and *The Passion of Christ*. Is it appropriate for them to view the harshness of reality in film form? We must also understand the criteria of the rating system is not objective. The film *Nowhere in Africa* was rated R for sexual content. This "sexual content" consisted of one or two non-sexual scenes in which the European characters adopt the local practice of going topless. Should this have the same rating as say, *Fifty Shades of Gray*?

This is something you, as the parent, have to decide. If it is appropriate for your daughter, and the content beneficial to teach her life reality, then the media should be considered. But it must also be an educated, well-thought-out decision.

Knowledge and understanding of entertainment content is always the goal of a Media Director. If we moms allow all influences into our daughters' lives, they will accept lifestyles and situational ethics that are contrary to what we want them to learn. But if we insulate them from all influence, they will be ill-prepared to make decisions independent from the insulation of their family instruction. The key is to stay involved, knowledgeable, and balanced in their consumption of the arts.

Influences from the inside

The fact that the world of entertainment terrifies so many in Middle America stunts the opportunity for change. This fear is just out of step with the need that exists. We must be willing to influence media from the inside by encouraging participation in the arts by our daughters and like-minded individuals who are passionate to become part of this community. When we disagree with the entertainment we are given, why not act to change it—instead of running from it in fear?

The key is to stay involved, knowledgeable, and balanced.

What if your daughter is one of those people destined to be a part of the entertainment industry? Then let her do it! Her talents and gifts may cry out in that direction, as our daughter Loren's did. Never let your fear deter your daughter from her destined path. If you have worked extremely hard the first eighteen years of her life to help her be the solid young woman she is capable of being, you have given her the tools she needs to change the media industry—for the good. She will find her way in this industry to ultimately impact not only the product delivered but the people with which she works. Why not make it better for her children, and her children's children?

Opening Minds to Possibilities

Television and film have also positively influenced young women, opening minds to possibilities not found in the small towns they grow up.

When I was young, I wanted to be Emma Peale—a British spy on the late 1960's television program, *The Avengers*. Much like Sydney Bristow in *Alias* or Annie Walker in *Covert Affairs*, Emma was beautiful, sophisticated, and hip. She had a great accent and could beat up any bad guy or girl who came along. She saved countries, friends, and foiled evil, with never a hair out of place. I wanted to be a spy: travel the world, defeat evil, and wear fantastic clothes. Not a thing wrong with those dreams. Though I didn't do what Emma did, just watching her made me believe anything was possible. That can't be all bad for a young girl.

After the turn of the century, viewers were reintroduced to classic books like *Lord of the Rings* and *Chronicles of Narnia* in film form. We have been reminded of historical moments of valor through *Saving Private Ryan*, *Braveheart*, and *Hacksaw Ridge*. We've been once again inspired now on the big screen by *Wonder Woman*. Movie-watching has been the mainstay for Friday and Saturday night entertainment. That's what you did with your friends, with your date, or in your family room.

Music is no different. The war songs from our parents' generation gave them courage and respite from difficult times. "Praise the Lord and Pass the Ammunition" was sung to me by my mother, but I never did get it. Praise the Lord and bullets— all in the same song? But for her generation, I believe it brought resolve and resilience in an extremely difficult time. Music has been a catalyst for racial and political change as well as portrayed love, loss, and celebration. It both commiserates on our sadness and marks occasions in which we delight.

I cannot leave this discussion of media without addressing that "only famous for acting stupid" stars of social media. Before you run out of the room screaming, "This has to be one of the most meaningless forms of entertainment *ever.*" remember this, much of it is not new. Through time there has been a genre of comedy called slapstick. Shakespeare wrote several of these same antics you see on iPhone screens into plays.

From *I Love Lucy* to *Home Alone* "acting stupid" has been a form of entertainment on stages and screens for a very long time. . Just because it currently comes in YouTube bites doesn't necessarily make it any less funny. It's simply being distributed in a different format. Creativity from many of the social media stars can be admired as they were in days past. Your concern as a parent is when it crosses from silliness to danger. Then a discussion is justly warranted.

I am a huge believer in the arts in all forms. Creative endeavors are magnificent! They provide color in a black-and-white world, and we should adamantly support them. Entertainment is a medium created to inspire and uplift. Let's do our best to make it become that again. We can succeed in pursuing that path by determining what is best for our daughters to partake in and purposefully avoiding what is not.

We must encourage our creative daughters to forge their roads within these industries. By their participation, they can change the culture in which we live.

If you take this job to successfully review and manage media, becoming a killer Media Director, your daughter will be well guided, your daughter's friends will be amazed at what you know, and future generations will be changed.

-5-

ACADEMIC ADVOCATE

| JOB DESCRIPTION |

Advocate on behalf of students in education programs and services. Responsible for working with the student and the academic system to help individuals select, outline, and achieve educational and developmental goals.

S CROLL THROUGH SOCIAL media feeds or turn on the television and you'll be confronted with a story on our failure in education. Students who can't read, low test scores, classes that are too large, subjects that are unlearned all seem to be evidence of a fruit-less system. The perceived need for money or more teachers, opening new schools and closing old ones, standardized testing for students and testing of teachers echo through the ongoing debate. We argue, set goals, make plans, spend more money; then argue, set goals, make plans, and spend more money again. Yet the stories appear, and the goals remain unmet.

There has to be an answer; we can't surrender our daughters to a failed system. We can't surrender any children to a failed system that is tasked to provide the education for future success. By allowing our children to remain in a quagmire that does not educate, instead often propagates, we defeat the purpose of schools altogether.

Such failure of education cannot be allowed to continue.

Let me suggest a mothering job that would *ensure* our students get educated. And the effects of this job will be best accomplished when compounded with other mothers committed to the same position. Envision with me what would terrify any school board in any county in America: a group of mothers—relentlessly determined to improve the school system their children attend—enter the chambers for the scheduled meetings. They listen, respond, and demand what is in the best interest of the *student,* not being concerned with the interest of the boards, nor the administration, nor even the teachers.

No other human is more motivated than we moms when it comes to educating our children. We are a powerful group with enormous ability and influence that enables us to do this job well, so we should use it. To make sure students are being taught, we mothers must be their Academic Advocate.

No other human is more motivated than we
moms when it comes to educating our children.

Some years ago, I watched a television interview with actress, Phylicia Rashad. This program aired in the early years of the daytime talk show *The View* and centered around a discussion regarding the plight of children in American education. The lack of learning, hope, and direction seemed rampant to the interviewer, Barbara Walters, and she was seeking a perspective from an actress she obviously admired. Anticipating the customary response of government intervention, new programs, and money undergirding the system, I was surprised at what I heard from Ms. Rashad.

She stated that no one is as effective in a child's life as their parents. Not educators, politicians, no one. Interestingly, she didn't differentiate between the needs of children born into wealth or poverty. In fact, when asked, she stated that both the wealthy parent and the impoverished parent are capable of great good or great harm. I wholeheartedly concur. Her focus was far from the typical platitudes that give responsibility to others, but she placed that burden directly upon the parents, stating that we should be "our children's advocate."

We are to be the one who represents and stands for our child's welfare. We are not to await help from anyone else; it is *our* duty to change for our children what needs to change.

To do this well, we have to understand the specifics of this job. I love the synonyms of the word *advocate*. An advocate is a supporter, backer, promoter, believer, activist, campaigner, and sponsor. The platform of education is the right one for us to be that person in our girl's life.

We can address and debate all kinds of issues about education, but when we put our daughter on that school bus or get in that carpool line for the first time, we don't want to waste our time or hers. Our girls are entering that school building to receive an education, nothing less. The goal must be to acquire tools to be a productive member of our society...simply to learn for life.

There is a system in place for that purpose—the American Education system—but it is far from perfect, and each school is an individual challenge. Knowing what you want for your daughter is one thing. But evaluating your school, then supporting and changing it, or choosing a different option, requires the activist in each of us.

As mothers, we fear the influences in our girls' lives—sexual pressure, driving a car, alcohol, and drugs, to name a few. We would never allow our daughters away from us seven hours a day with no real understanding of what they are doing, who is caring for them, how they are being affected, and what good is coming from those hours. But we often do this with their education.

Is your daughter being taught what she needs to learn to become a woman of purpose? Do you know the teachers who are educating her? Are these educators instilling merely academics, or also theories and philosophies in their curriculum that might go against your values? Do the academics required of your daughter fit the needs and talents she possesses?

Building Your Knowledge Base

My husband and I have built three homes, one office building, and remodeled a fourth home. The tasks each time were daunting. Even though we weren't wielding the nail gun, from beginning to end, they required a lot of effort on our part. Imagine when building a home that you meet a person someone else sent into your life to take care of this task for you. You spend forty-five minutes in a room with that person along with twenty-five other couples he is building for as well, and he tells the whole group how the year is going to go. After that brief meeting, you give him your cash, then drive away, never seeing the builder again until you return to your site and the house is completed.

It's preposterous to think you'd leave a project like that with just anyone who pulled up in a pickup truck removing their tool belts from their vehicles to begin labor on your home. You haven't seen the detailed plans. You don't know the location of the windows, let alone the room sizes, plumbing fixtures, and electrical outlets. If you want to make sure your home is well built, you'd meet and interview the workman, define the role they would play, and sign a contract way before the first piece of dirt was moved to lay the foundation.

You'd also need to be confident that these people knew their trade—that they were prepared to build the home you wanted with the materials and craftsmanship you expected. You would never want to drive up to your completed home, crafted by people you know nothing about, and find the surprises: the leaking roof, the clogged sinks, and the cracked flooring.

But in the building of the knowledge base of our daughters, we often do exactly that. We don't know the teachers, the classes, or the education they are receiving. We have a forty-five-minute meeting at the beginning of the year and return at the end of the school year to pick up our children for summer vacation.

Okay, so there are parent-teacher conferences if needed. But if your child is not making waves, you may not get called in. Perhaps you attend a play, sporting event, or a concert. But as a parent, that is not enough. You must be involved in the substance of education, supporting and defining it along the way.

Three Fault Lines in Education

To do this well, you must understand the three fault lines in education:

› The academic focus lacks understanding of the diversity of human talent.

› The culturally relevant education has an emphasis on cultural revolutions, feeling and philosophy, not fact.

› The system doesn't offer a practical education—one that meets the needs of day-to-day life.

Every student should be given the opportunity and be expected to read, write, and master math problems. Every student should be given the opportunity and expected to learn discipline in study, achievement, and mastery of skills, knowledge of factual history to understand their world, and a view of their country's inception, purpose and privilege. We should also know when reviewing our school teachers and school administrators that not all are incompetent, having an ulterior agenda, or uncompassionate.

My daughters have had the privilege of being taught by many teachers who are both compassionate and valiantly committed to their craft. The instruction Loren and Chelsea received from these teachers was magnificent and will forever enrich their lives.

Chelsea's chosen career is that of an elementary teacher within the public-school system. It has been through her insights I that have become acutely aware of the challenges faced by teachers who are there to do what we desire, teach our children well. Her career comes with no fewer trials than the entertainment business my elder daughter works in, yet it pays a whole lot less.

I will stand and defend these warriors in education as ardently as I will work to change a flawed system. Recognizing and supporting the successes in education are as important as addressing the faults. As we examine the changes we can make, let's do it with reason.

Fault line #1: The inability to educate the diverse.

Diversity is a word bandied about in contemporary conversations, but that's not the general definition of diversity that I want to address. This discussion is not about race, gender, height, weight, or even nose size. I believe those conversations lose the exquisiteness of our most beautiful diversity, our many and differing talents, gifts, and abilities—all wonderfully complementary! Math, English, and science aren't the only talents we find in girls. Humans possess all kinds of delightful, creative, and unique abilities—talents that need attention to develop.

I was a mere fourteen years of age when I made my personal education disclaimer. Not understanding at the time why I did it, I found myself actively making my own path.

"No, Bob Hinkle isn't my brother."

You see, my name was Darlene Hinkle, so logic would have it that somehow, we came from the same gene pool. Yet this is the sentence that began my freshman year of high school. I said it to every educator at my high school. These were the teachers who had committed to educating students, opening their eyes to possibilities and infusing them with knowledge. I'm sure they thought I was truly crazy when the first thing out of my mouth after raising my hand for attendance was: "In case you're curious, I don't know Bob Hinkle."

In every class, I attended I made this proclamation. On my first visit to the school office I told the secretaries at their desks, "Bob Hinkle, you know him? Well, I don't." I'm quite sure I even sang it down the halls just to make sure it was understood. You see, these people frightened me. They had expectations I had no intention of meeting.

I have this older brother four years my senior. I love him very much, but he was, and is, really smart. Bob was the kind of guy who of course took Calculus and Trigonometry because he could; perhaps he enjoyed them. That would be foreign to me. When he went to college, he majored in engineering, experimenting in which kind he would like to pursue—electrical, architectural, aeronautical, civil, and whatever engineering they offered that I had not a clue.

Bob can read almost anything and retain the most profound information. He is one of the most well-read, well-studied, and able to approach every subject from a basis of knowledge humans I know. He is also gracious, kind, and a great guy.

But in high school, I saw all of this intelligence as a stumbling block in the path I wanted to take. I didn't want the pressure of having to be smart too, so I chose the easy road. I lied. Bob had already graduated, so it was a simple statement. I told myself I could pull this off and make my path to the land of higher education. It was also the path of least resistance.

I'm a person who is focused (my husband calls it stubborn), yet I say I'm merely tenacious. I don't give up on commitments. While in high school I made personal pledges. They included ensuring that there were enough study halls in my school day to never bring work home. I graduated having achieved this goal. I decided to, at all costs, avoid the intense math and sciences, choosing instead to take music, art, psychology, composition, and any class known as a "fluff course." Such courses were my education mainstay. I only took what I had to, to get my degree for potential college admittance because my parents wanted to make sure I didn't forsake all life options by my "tenacious" commitments.

I didn't want the pressure of having to be smart too, so I chose the easy road. I lied.

My senior year was the greatest. My school had a work-study program that was a very real-world form of education. But for me, it was prison furlough. I could get out of school before noon and go to a job where I was paid real money at the same time I was getting high school credit.

What a plan! Leave school early, eat lunch wherever you want, and go to a job that isn't that hard because the people are kind and don't expect much from a high school senior. And while working, I was completing my high school education. Then, as an added bonus, I got to take a midday break from my work when my boyfriend could meet me and take a thirty-minute ride on his motorcycle. Life was good.

All of this information was kept secret from my daughters for a very long time. Did I want them to follow in their mother's footsteps? I think not.

Was it the best plan for a high school education? Not even.

Did my deceit lead to my betterment? What do you think?

Traditional education isn't right for everyone. I'm not excusing my own choices in high school, but I realize now that they were not all wrong on my part. I was not Bob Hinkle. I was Darlene Hinkle. Math was not my primary talent; I was creative. When so many students were intrigued by the possibilities of math formulas, I was visualizing an entire play in my mind. I was creating and sewing unique items of clothing and then daring to wear them in public. Music played in my mind constantly.

While I'm not recommending we allow our daughters to take the path of least resistance, I am advising that as Academic Advocates it is our job to make sure they receive the education appropriate to their talents. When they have to take a predetermined number of math, science, and English classes for college entrance, what time do we allow for the arts? And time isn't the only issue. The lack of variety of programs in our schools is a disservice as well. When looking for jobs that require creativity, you may be surprised at how numerous they are.

In the world of television and film, there are hundreds of jobs for the individuals possessing an array of talents. Screen-writing, acting, directing, producing, editing, and operating cameras are all careers to fulfill that part of the entertainment world. There are talent agents, television network employees, film company personnel, animators, costumers, musicians, set designers, and special effects creators that all take part in the finished product we see on the small and large screen.

Then you take the world of music. Songwriters, publishers, musicians, studio engineers, managers, performers, singers, record company employees, engineers, publicists, studio owners, album cover designers, video producers, directors, and scores of others are essential to the creation and distribution of the music we love.

We can't forget about art, photography, theater, clothing design, books, and the lists go on. Our world would be sterile without creativity. How boring buildings would look if they were left only to minds filled with actualities, not possibilities. Design or art is such a vital part of our world. We have to ask ourselves if we are nurturing the creative talents as much as we are cultivating the scientific and mathematical abilities. We spend so much time working on the brain we lose the heart and soul.

My niece, Shanna, is smart, really smart. She took her first ACT when she was thirteen and tested better than most high school seniors. She has gone on to score in high school the perfect five on advanced placement tests in mathematics. She is the academically off the chart member of our family.

Through the years we took a lot of trips together. Spring breaks were some of our favorites. Our family owned this big red conversion van. It was great for traveling, because it was full size, with room for up to seven people. All back and middle seats had headphone jacks that would attach to the television, CD player, or car radio. That meant each kid traveling with us could choose her preferred entertainment. Life was wonderful during those trips because the front seats, where we adults sat, were quiet. Not the normal "when are we getting there?", "how much longer?" Or other questions when you still have miles to go until you reach your destination. We adults could relax, talk to each other, or nap (if we weren't the driver), and just focus on the road ahead.

My girls would be busy with their music or movies. But Shanna? She'd often be found working in a book—and not just any book, but a math brain-teaser book, designed to make math more complex and challenging. Shanna loved them. To me, these books represented work—a painful exercise not ever undertaken by choice, something to avoid at all costs. But to Shanna, it was fun.

God wired Shanna's brain to love math; she has since become a computer programmer. I'm so glad he did. Without intellects like hers, the creative people would not have the cameras, computers, software, studios, electronics, and all the other types of technology that are necessary in today's world to create and distribute their art. And if it were not for the creative people, the mathematicians and engineers would be limited in need for their innovations. Their world would lack color. To build a computer only for math or science and not for graphic art, image generation, animation, editing, or music recording would be developing a sterile technology.

Difficult math and science subjects are appropriate for those, like Shanna, who are destined for those careers. But never should they be the only life route, nor should they be the only praise-worthy endeavor in education. If your creative daughter makes C's or D's in math and is working her very best, then her best should be good enough. If her talents are in the arts, applaud them, as well as nurture and develop. As in every part of life, identify your daughter's abilities, understand them, and support her. Never let traditional education defeat your daughter.

Recognizing there are students like Shanna and students like I was and providing for varied talents is crucial to a well-rounded education system. It's also imperative for advocating effectively for your daughter. Redirecting some academic emphasis and requirements from the core subjects to the creative subjects is one necessary step toward a diverse education. It's also one area that the effective Academic Advocate relentlessly pursues with the school board.

Fault line #2: The emphasis on feeling, philosophy, and cultural relevance instead of the instruction of facts.

I love the statement of Sherwood Anderson, renowned author of American literature in the early 1900s, regarding education. "The whole object of education is...to develop the mind. The mind should be a thing that works." That's certainly simple enough, isn't it? We are led to believe the education system is lofty and above common man…when it is not. If the brain works, the information provided in teaching form should be enough. It should not have to be interpreted, diffused, or in any way construed as anything other than fact. The mind doesn't need development; it only needs fact-based instruction.

I recently noticed a change in education when it comes to history. It has evolved into a non-messy and content-selective subject in our school system. When history is cleaned up and sanitized, it is no longer history. The study of our human past, filled with faults, mistakes, and complicated individuals speaks of those who did great wrong and those who did inordinately right. History is filled with the evil as well as the valiant acts of humankind. Putting history under a foggy lens, trying to make it politically correct or slanted toward cultural justice, is a disservice to our children.

History today is often re-written to justify a political or cultural agenda. Focusing on or eliminating parts of a historical account with the purpose of achieving the desired perception is equally damaging. It is easy to present your viewpoint within the prism of history when you choose to tell only part of a story. To learn life lessons, you have to know and understand the past mistakes and great acts of every race, culture, and individuals represented in the tale. You also have to recognize the consequences of their actions.

The educators that have chosen to provide a culturally relative education are missing the reality of what educating is. Learning all information just as it is and gaining insight from that knowledge enables the student to determine how she wants to live.

Culturally relevant education holds to the thinking that the education system will provide what society deems to be useful and needful.

Following World War II American education strayed from pure education (the simple facts) to the functions of solving society's problems—poverty, pollution, urban unrest, crime, and any other malady the institution felt needed addressing. This began mainly in the universities of the time because government grants were being given out to professors who taught classes on how to remedy the cultural issues of society. Each time a social ill was addressed by the professor, the possibility of an infusion of government dollars came into that department. This climate created a diversion from the teaching of factual information to the *interpretation* of that information. No longer were the instructors in place for, or even paid for, the instruction of fact. Instead, they became entitled and even obligated to dispense opinion to the students.

Therefore, amidst education fact, one will find information spun to support a professor's theory, correct a perceived wrong, and change the views of the listeners. What's wrong with that? It's opinion, an individual's thought. The conclusions are often based on false assumptions, from a background that is culturally different from your own; yet, coming from an instructor, they are dispensed with authority. A student relies on a teacher for correct, unbiased information—not theory. The presentation of theory should only be a line of reasoning that is in no way provable or is potentially inerrant, not as conclusive.

The issue with culturally relative education is that it is backward. Conclusions are taught before instilling the information that led to the development of the conclusion. The *students* are the ones who should form the conclusions, not their instructors.

If taught in science about the world of botany, without the teacher editorials that usually go along with it, the student who loved the beauty of plants and the scientific interrelation of the vegetative life would naturally follow the path of maintaining and protecting plant life. Now that's ecology in motion!

The students are the ones who should form the conclusions, not their instructors.

If taught the messiness of history with slavery, genocide, battle, as well as educated about the defenders of freedom, the liberator students who were activists by nature would find their cause and purpose. Equality would be advanced, injustice addressed, and the defenseless defended. Before the culturally relative period of education, many wrongs were righted, downtrodden were lifted up, and human compassion advanced, a need was seen, and a purposed heart ignited.

The education system then found itself advancing from trying to answer corporate problems to address the therapeutic needs of the students. Many educators felt the need to cope with the students' "identity crisis" and resolve emotional conflict. Creating an aggressive thrust toward a student's self-awareness—feeling good about who you are and achieving for yourself in this culturally relevant education system.

At first glance, it sounds good, doesn't it? You don't want your daughter to feel bad about herself, do you?

Well, yes, you do, feeling bad about yourself—knowing you can achieve more, be kinder than you've been, and work harder than you have—is part of improving as a human. Self-disappointment is a vital emotion. Your daughter will be better if she thinks she needs to. While teaching the feel-good philosophy, schools don't promote kindness, humility, compassion, personal ethics, and integrity. They instead create a selfish atmosphere where the mind and self, is valued over all other achievements.

You may think it's not the schools' purpose to teach humility, but why not? They are teaching pride. And what about ethics? Shouldn't the concept of ethics be interwoven in achievement? As education has "progressed" a mindset that truth is fluid, right is relative has evolved primarily in the world of higher education. This trend has served to not only confuse a generation but denigrate humanity to our lowest form.

There is a right and a wrong. There are truth and lies. Principles understood at the core of human achievement, or all other instruction taught will fail miserably.

If your daughter doesn't do her homework, it's not okay. If she doesn't study for the test, she should receive a failing grade, even if doesn't make her "feel good." After all, she earned it. Personal responsibility in education teaches humility. Consequences for actions are necessary for real-life advances.

Fault line #3: The lack of instruction to prepare the student for life in the real world.

This is why it's so vital to you, Mom, to be your daughter's Academic Advocate. Historically, education has been the only means to a life that would otherwise be unlikely. It's the tunnel from poverty to position, from lack of accomplishment and failure to success. For many, it's the only way they have to leave the past and create a hopeful future.

That's the way it was for Mary McLeod Bethune. Born July 10, 1875, two years before the end of the Reconstruction (the time after the Civil War that slaves were given new lives), Mary and her family still lived in poverty.

When she was nine years old, Mary tagged along with her mother to take a basket of freshly washed and ironed clothes to her former master Ben Wilson's house. They had to go around the home to the entrance in the rear, the one through which the blacks could enter. In 1884 in Mayesville, South Carolina, there was absolute segregation between the races. Her mother went inside to take the family their clothes and receive the few cents paid for such a job.

Waiting outside, Mary was captivated by a children's playhouse she saw and peeked inside. Two white girls about her age sat inside on scaled-down furniture. They were playing with their dolls.

"Hello, Mary! Do you want to come in?" one of them called out. Of course, she did. Mary was just a little girl, and she wasn't admitted to such circles every day. From this simple act of playing together, a passion ignited in Mary that day. Seeing past her circumstances and limitations, she made a decision that changed her life and the lives of many after her.

You see, Mary was the fifteenth child of seventeen children. She was the first child born free to a family of former slaves. Her family only knew hard work, cotton fields, and grim times. They were free and had five acres of land to work but nothing more.

Mary wanted more, and this day made her determine how to go about it. She recounted the event in this manner:

I picked up one of the books…. And one of the girls said to me—"You can't read that—put that down. I will show you some pictures over here," and when she said to me, "You can't read that—put that down," it just did something to my pride and to my heart that made me feel that someday I would read just as she was reading.

Mary McLeod Bethune discovered the world of education through that one act. She realized the lack of education created the plight of her race, and she begged her parents for that opportunity. It came when the Mission Board of the Presbyterian Church sent one young black woman, Emma Wilson, in city clothes to educate the black children of South Carolina. Mary was the first to attend. She graduated from that school at age twelve, wanting more education but not having any way to achieve it. She prayed for a miracle.

A few years later Mary was awarded a scholarship that had been given by a Quaker woman in Colorado. She had life savings she wanted to donate to allow one black child a chance to attend Scotia Seminary School in North Carolina. Mary became that child. After attending Scotia Seminary, she received a scholarship to the Moody Bible Institute in Chicago, where she continued to be a high achiever. Mary was the only American black student in attendance, and one of only a few non-whites.

But Mary didn't stop with her education. After graduating from Moody Bible Institute, she moved to Daytona, Florida, where she began her school in 1904: The Literary and Industrial School for Training Negro Girls. The beginnings were meager. Mary had only $1.50 to her name, five students, and shipping crates for desks. But she had a determined heart. Mary created opportunity through education for many that would not have received it anywhere else. She had immense faith in God and believed that nothing was impossible. She remained president of the school for more than forty years.

Mary had only $1.50 to her name, five students, and shipping crates for desks. But she had a determined heart.

While much of her energy was devoted to keeping the College solvent, she also provided a better living condition for her parents and an education for her son and grandson. Two axioms of Mary's philosophy, "not for myself, but for others" and "I feel that as I give I get" were confessed to Charles S. Johnson.

In 1954, she attended the World Assembly for Moral Re-Armament, an organization that subscribed to the principles Mary McLeod Bethune had lived by: "absolute honesty, absolute purity, absolute unselfishness, and absolute love."

For Mary, education was her tunnel to success. This is a story of the life education can create when it remains pure, teaching students to become better persons in every sense. Mary learned the academics, but as she became the teacher, she also taught love, faith, selflessness, and striving toward a better world.

Mary Bethune's education was practical for her time. Today we moms need to determine what is practical for our daughters. Our girls live in a world where they drive cars, buy insurance, receive credit cards, apply for mortgages, get credit ratings, fill out applications, make resumes, cook food, file tax returns, and bring up children. Are these things part of today's instruction?

My younger daughter learned calculus to complete her fourth year of high school math for college entrance. I'll bet real money that's not the class she uses the most now that she's out on her own. Her sophomore year the school she attended offered an elective course on consumer math, educating students on auto insurance, credit ratings, bank reconciliation, mortgage rates, and more. I was insistent this was a course she should take because I knew it was what she would need for real life. You cannot exist in America today without understanding credit, interest, insurance, banking, and many other daily tasks. Yet, Algebra II, Calculus, and more are core classes—not consumer math.

Early in reviewing schools, I was taken aback when meeting with one high school guidance counselor. I asked if they offered a consumer math course. He replied they did, but it wasn't important for the student to take.

Colleges would consider it an "easy class," and it wouldn't look good on my daughter's transcript. I replied that it might not prepare her for college entrance, but it would for life—especially since she'd be spending many more years living in the real world than she would in college. He looked at me as if I didn't get it, but I think he was the clueless one.

In the past, auto shop and home economics were standard educational fare. Should we not rethink those programs and any others that may be appropriate? We should add vocational schools and community college education and place it on the same level as other secondary institutions. There should not be any pomposity on behalf of the higher learning academic over practical learning. The offerings vocational schools and community colleges offer are just as effective as the four-year institutions.

I'd love to see a professor of philosophy with a lofty attitude left without the local auto mechanic or dental hygienist. Broken-down cars and bad teeth would certainly get his attention. No one can philosophize his way off the side of the interstate when the car doesn't run. Perhaps in the absence of help when he was without a running vehicle, he'd begin to place appropriate value on these trades and treat them with the same respect and dignity he did his own course of studies.

I'd love to see a professor of philosophy with a lofty attitude left without the local auto mechanic or dental hygienist.

Above all, we need to reinstitute hope—hope for the future, integrated with faith. Yes, the *faith* word. To believe there is someone greater than we are and more competent shouldn't be that scary to most people. On the contrary, it should bring reassurance. We are often so afraid of alienating the individual that we deny the populace hope. Where are our children without it? This world is a difficult place to live, with hurt and heartache on every side. Our children are not shielded from it. Teaching the principles,

Bethune had lived by—"absolute honesty, absolute purity, absolute unselfishness, and absolute love"—will offer hope where needed the most.

You may find your options are limited, the community in which you live doesn't offer the things you know are appropriate for your child. Perhaps one day it will change but that day may not be soon enough. Homeschool or private school, don't be afraid to look at all the alternatives that will offer the education uniquely appropriate for you and your girl. You will also discover there will be seasons to your daughter's educational path, institutions that may be appropriate one year may not in be another. As an advocate understanding, this is part of the job.

But if the public-school system is your only option, here are tips shared by my daughter, as a teacher in the public-school system:

›   Start by being and staying involved.

›   Communicate consistently with her teacher, even if you don't get a status report, you should ask for one.

›   Partner with the teacher in your girl's education, tackling the challenges together.

›   Help with homework and school responsibilities for a season, then over time let them become the one who is responsible, to grow their independence.

›   Expose your girl to different experiences and real-life training. This will build their basis of knowledge that will undergird their academic performance.

Then here's your final challenge. The next time the school board and public officials state that the teachers will lose their jobs because of a budget shortfall. Assemble your group of Academic Advocate mothers. Have the ones whose talents are research and numbers find the financial breakdown of the school system. Then allow the creative members of your group to take that information to create posters, charts, and presentation materials. The members of your group who love networking and public speaking can contact other mothers, local media, and address the school board.

What will this exercise prove? It's not the classroom that has the enormous amount of waste; it's the *administration*. That's where the spending cuts need to land. You will indeed expose some of the fallacy in their dialogue (and scare them a little into hopefully making the right choices for the sake of the children).

As Academic Advocates, let's take the words of Herbert Spencer, British philosopher and sociologist, to heart" "The great aim of education is not knowledge, but action." If we moms commit to affect the school system we find our girls in, it *will be* changed, one school at a time—for our daughters and their daughters as well.

-6-

PROFESSOR OF GENDER STUDIES

| JOB DESCRIPTION |

Educator of the interdisciplinary study of the complex connection between sexes; providing a curriculum that explores and debates gender as one of the most fundamental facts of our existence. Fosters critical thinking in the role of feminism and gender identity. Must create in the student an understanding of the significance and the effect of political, economic, and social systems in society.

J UST IN CASE you thought this mom job title was made up and doesn't exist in the real world, it's not, and it does. This lofty, highbrow position is a real job at most universities. The course descriptions at these institutions at times sounding somewhat vague and innocuous, but I can assure you the content isn't. Our universities, as well as our culture, are working overtime to tell young women who they are, what they should think about themselves, what role in life their gender should play and that gender itself is a fluid term. Their goal is to ultimately instill in them their acceptable definition and roles of a female, as well as the interpretation or confusion of what gender is.

I can also assure you that this information has very little to do with your daughter's well-being and positive self-concept. There is another agenda actively at work. With "experts" intent on providing this instruction, you simply have to be the one who gets there first. *You* must be the first person to educate your daughter in Gender Studies, "providing a curriculum that explores and debates gender as one of the most fundamental facts of our existence."

Your daughter needs to know how to live well and delight in, the unique nature of being a female. She needs to understand what is "equality" in the genders and how to interact gracefully with the opposite sex. She must comprehend the good, the bad, and the ugly of female characteristics. She must also understand gender can be defined biologically as well as emotionally. Consider yourself officially enrolled in the curriculum required to obtain your doctorate in Gender Studies.

Your daughter needs to understand what is true "equality" in the genders and how to gracefully interact with the opposite sex.

Every doctorate requires time and research, then ends with a lengthy dissertation. For the mother version of this degree, life provides you the time to gain the education needed. The required research comes from your observation of human nature. The mother's dissertation then comes orally—presented repeatedly to the audience and also to the absolute dismay of our very own girls. What you do not need is a heady team of educators to perform a research project or a government grant to fund it; you just need a bit of information and common sense.

This chapter will provide the information you'll need to support your position, as well as historical views with current analysis. You will understand the role of feminism, positive and negative, as well as the definition of gender.

But the conclusions most convincing are those made by observing the unique nature, grace, and strength of women who have lived before us. On the subject of female equality, those ladies, by living, understood how to be the strong women they were created to be.

A Grand Lady of Grit and Grace

Minnie Ethel Maness Brock, or better known by the family as "Minnie Mom," was my husband's paternal grandmother. This grand lady was made up of *grit* and *grace*. It was an honor to sit with her, gleaning vast amounts of wisdom. She was a Southern woman who lived most of her life in the mountains of Kentucky. Rearing eight children on very little money with a husband who worked on the railroad or at the sawmill, she raised everything they ate, sewed everything they wore, and worked harder than an American steelworker just to keep her family afloat.

When I met her, she was well into her seventies, with a completely white afro—the big, curly kind that sprouted in every direction. Minnie Mom was probably five-foot-seven and maybe 130 pounds. She was a little stooped but mighty. The year the roofers worked on her home, she climbed the ladder to join them. Whether it was because she thought they weren't doing the job the way she wanted, or she was bringing them something to drink, we were unsure. It was probably both. But much to our dismay, this eighty-plus-year-old woman was on the roof.

What I was most in awe of was her wisdom. Minnie Mom's comments were always sage. She'd seen so much of life. When we visited with her in Kentucky following the birth of our second daughter, her advice to me was: "Two children are quite enough. God gave us two hands and two legs, so two is enough to handle."

Knowing she had several more than that, I asked, "But Minnie Mom, you had eight kids."

Her wry reply? "Yes, I did." With that simple statement, she said everything she meant to say.

One of her most poignant stories came to me on a day that she and I were discussing politics during the year of a presidential election. Knowing her age, I asked her when she began voting. Apparently, like most young women of her generation, she registered for this privilege soon after she got married. She joined the same party as her husband, whom I knew of as "Poppy" (he had passed away years prior), each year casting her vote in tandem with him...until the year of the "no account sheriff," that is.

"Two children are quite enough. God gave us two hands and two legs; two is enough to handle.
—MINNIE MOM

This local election included a county sheriff she didn't like. Questioning her husband about this particular candidate, Minnie Mom found Poppy adamant. This sheriff was the representative of the party to which they belonged, and of course, he would get their votes. So, Minnie Ethel Brock voted as she always had, with her husband.

Not long after the sheriff was elected, shady deals he was involved with came to light. He accepted money he shouldn't have, to do something he wasn't supposed to do. The constituents responded slowly, but respond they did. When reelection came, he was resoundingly voted out of office. Even though her husband cast his vote straight party line, including for that sheriff, Minnie Mom broke ranks. As she put it, "Wasn't about to see that no-account sheriff in office anymore."

That was the year she vowed never again to vote for someone just because it was expected. When she told me that story with a sparkle in her eye, I believed that, for Minnie Brock, it was her Independence Day. This was not an act of rebellion or defiance; I never heard a word of disrespect or disparity toward her husband. Nothing changed in their relationship. Her workload remained the same, and the struggles weren't any less. But

Minnie Mom had insight about how to make independent decisions, and she became comfortable doing so. She grew as a woman in that year, adding acceptable independence to all her other life roles.

Changing Times

The years each of my daughters turned eighteen held a presidential election. They could not have imagined anyone denying them their day in the voting booth. It wasn't until 1920 that women received voting rights. The fact that our gender would not have been allowed this privilege seems unbelievable. However, many historical rights previously denied to women in America were won by strong, determined activists. Land ownership, property rights, education, career opportunity, and that right to vote are only a few. These changes in their time were necessary, but that was then, and this is now.

Times have indeed changed. To prove that, let me give you a few statistics. In the year 2015 according to the National Center for Education Statistics[1], 57.2% of Bachelor degrees and 59.9% of Master degrees awarded were given to women. Based upon research statistics in 2015 provided by the National Association of Women Business Owners[2], more than 9.4 million businesses were owned by women, employing 7.9 million people. In that year alone, these women-led businesses generated $1.5 trillion in sales.

The earnings ratio of women to men has seen annual increases from 1990 to date. While I agree we have not achieved equal pay for all positions, nor opportunities in all careers, studies show that the pay disparity touted within the halls of feminism is false in its premise. The variables that include career choice, the percentage of women working within the higher-paying industries, and the number of hours worked are often not entered into the calculations. Instead of the often-heard twenty percent disparity, the gap is much closer to six percent.

I cite these statistics because you need to know them. While any gap needs addressing, unlike the women before us, we currently have the opportunity to do so. We, as women, have won our rights and have everything we need to succeed on the home front, in the workplace, in the political arena, with land ownership, and in so many other areas. It may not come effortlessly, nor without hurdles, yet because the opportunities are achievable, I wonder why are so many females still unhappy and dissatisfied?

The Subtle Costs of Feminism

Feminism, by definition, is the theory that men and women should be equal politically, economically, and socially. The advocacy of women's rights through the equality of sexes is a philosophy that is easy to agree with. Equality between genders is true and right. Even so, current feminism stances have not held an allure for me. I have never felt inferior to a man, nor have I reared my daughters to feel inferior. Neither do I think a man should feel inferior to a woman. If feminism is simply about equality, I am on board. Equality is that we are on the same playing field of life—equal in talents and opportunity.

Equal—or superior?

However, I am convinced that the platform of women's rights today doesn't care as much about *equal* rights as it does achieving *superior* rights. Take time to research their current agendas, and you'll find they include abortion, liberalism, lesbianism, and independence from, as well as power over, men. The irony is that these stances take place at the same time we acknowledge men have used their position to have superiority over their female counterparts. Sexual harassment has often been allowed because men traditionally had higher level opportunities than women, and in some industries, still do. While this is entirely unacceptable, I don't believe seeking retaliation by placing ourselves in a superior position is the answer either. It is teaching our daughters how to be confident and capable in all scenarios that will create equality.

It is teaching our daughters how to be confident and capable in all scenarios that will create equality.

In your research, observe the generation of daughters that followed this age of the feminist. One of the early goals was that women no longer be viewed as a sex object. This admirable desire was for women to be respected and rewarded for their abilities, instead of being regarded through the prism of sex.

But what has transpired? Contrary to the stated goal, young ladies today have mastered the art of getting attention from their sexuality. The movement didn't change the power of sex or the innate ability for a young woman to understand and use that power. Instead, it often failed to teach a daughter how to cultivate an appropriate, successful relationship with a man. The alternatives presented were to argue with, belittle, or manipulate our male counterparts. When the next generation realized those alternatives didn't work well, they fell back to sex.

Identical—or different?

The second irony is that the movement created confusion. In attempting to be *equal,* we have mistakenly sought to be *identical.* By working for equal opportunities, we have come to believe that we are equal to men in nature, ability, and desires. The brilliant part of the gender differences is that we are indeed different!

I can't help but cite a 2003 BBC News story entitled "What are the 78 differences between women and men?[3]" The article was written several years ago, yet it is still true today.

To get ideas flowing, four BBC participants added their thoughts, funny and enlightening.

Women have the "if you need to be told, I'm not going to tell you" gene.

—David Bergin Switzerland

Men have a gene that enables them to maintain a vice-like grip on the remote control while reclining on the sofa studying the insides of the eyelids.

—Jane, UK

Men like to have all their stuff (DVDs, CDs, etc.) on show to impress their mates. Women like to hide things in cupboards.

—Mark Nelson, UK

Women put things on the bottom stair to take up next time she has to go upstairs. Men just step over them until told to pick them up.

—Karen Kelsey, UK

Women can use sex to get what they want. Men cannot, as sex is what they want.

—Steve Munoz, US

These observations are endless, unscientific, and a testament to the fact that we don't need a government study or a doctorate to teach us we are different. We all get it. Live just a little bit of time relating to the opposite sex, and it becomes abundantly clear.

There is a recent addition to the Gender Studies discussion that requires our attention—the fluid interpretation of gender itself. When entering this debate, we cannot ignore the science. "The New Sex Scorecard" in *Psychology Today*[4] in 2003 spoke of these physical and psychological differences. This study, while looking at the biology of male XY chromosomes versus the female XX chromosomes, went a little further and studied the gray matter of our brains. Did you know that women have 15 to 20 percent more gray matter—the ability for processing vast amounts of information—than men? While men have larger brains than women, their brain mass has a larger percentage of white matter. A more recent study by Cambridge University[5] confirmed the disparity in brain tissue. White matter provides spatial reasoning, which is singlemindedness—the ability to focus and conquer life's tasks. Interestingly, white matter also is less easily damaged than gray matter.

These scientific facts are summed up in the following hypothetical scenario. Husband and wife are on a street corner in New York City. A mugger approaches. The wife, while seeing the cute red dress in the store window to her left, is impatiently waiting for the walk sign to illuminate, observing the family in the cab with the little boy wiggling anxiously, and simultaneously deciding what she will eat for dinner. The husband is concentrating on safely getting him and his wife back to the hotel to catch the end of the ball game.

Mugger approaches, husband immediately reacts to defend, focused on stopping the event. Wife observes mugger's eye color and height, clings to purse, worries about the husband, and wonders how the children will get along without them. Mugger hits husband in the head, where he gets less damage than the wife would, knocks him down, and runs off with wife's purse. The wife is screaming every detail that just took place and searching for someone to call 911. As she bends down to care for her husband, she's still thinking about the children back home and wondering whether they'll make their dinner reservation.

The moral of this story is that these reactions and responses created by our nature are tremendously complementary. To confuse the truth of both gender equality and gender identity belies both scientific and empirical evidence. Looking at our humanity in the early years, a man could venture out into the forest and hunt more effectively and aggressively than a woman. One hour out in the woods without spotting dinner in moving form would lead most women to say, "Enough of that. I've got other things to do." But a woman can cook breakfast, dress for work, call the plumber, review homework, and bark orders to the children all at the same time.

One hour out in the woods without spotting dinner in moving form would lead most women to say, "Enough of that. I've got other things to do."

Just because I use these examples doesn't mean I'm relegating women to these roles. Instead, it is to show that we as women were *created to multitask*. Additionally, a man is more instinctively the provider and family protector while the woman is the nurturer and caregiver.

And now my challenge to our feminist friends: Why is this a bad thing? While scientists are still debating what this means, there is undeniable evidence of the uniqueness of each gender. And those "uniquenesses" are exceptional, and downright good things!

So, let me ask you: assuming the women's movement achieved its goals of equality, which I believe in the case of equal opportunity, it has. It leads one to ponder if these changes have ensured our betterment.

Take a quick look at the realities. The relationship between the sexes, which was to be much improved by the movement, has disintegrated. Women may be getting paid better, but we are not being treated better. The recent exposure of sexual harassment and sexual abuse in the workplace serves as a glaring example of this truth.

The divorce rate is higher, domestic violence is rampant, and relationship commitments are absent, all indicators that the women's movement has failed. By accepting the premise that equal means identical and that gender is a term left to interpretation, we have lost a sharp definition of our complementary natures. We have also belittled the value of the men in a woman's life. We believe we no longer need them. We deem we can do and be everything they can…and sometimes better.

By accepting the premise that equal means identical, we have belittled the value of the men in a woman's life.

Professor Mom, the truth is we cannot. By taking from a man a part of their very nature, we have left them feeling unfulfilled. A man wants and *needs* to be the protector and provider. They need to hunt the game, which translates in our world today as having a job that provides for the family.

Although there are men today, whose life goal appears to become a member of Peter Pan's lost boy club. You will find that their discontentment and lack of commitment stems from denying the nature they possess. Their innermost desire *is* to be the defender of their wives and children. Keeping the family from harm's way is instinctual and part of every man's nature. A man needs to be the hero. Whether we women like to admit it or not, we love and need a hero, too.

Women always need to be needed. When we are bettering someone else's life, we are happiest. Whether it is husband, children, coworker, parents, or friends, we feel fulfilled when we can help. That means the nature and the needs of men and women are complementary. The way to achieve harmony in families is by embracing and respecting these differences. That's why a mother and a father in this harmonizing relationship provide the best instruction in their children's lives.

Several years ago, I saw a very real-world representation of the differences of gender. A television program had created a waiting room scenario, placing a hidden camera in the wall of the room. First, the mother and child entered the room. Then later, separately, the father and that same child followed suit; what happened next obliterated all conjecture on how the sexes would fill their time.

The mother entered, looked at the books on the table, and spoke softly to her child, discussing which book to read. Upon making that decision, the child crawled into the mother's lap, opened the book, and together they spent time reading each page. The children sat quietly, twisting their hair or sucking their thumbs, attentive to the stories in front of them. If they didn't go for the book, the mothers chose the puzzles on the coffee table. Turning the board upside down, she would assist her child in placing the pieces correctly into the spaces created. Each of these exercises ended with the mother holding her child in her lap and cuddling.

Later, the father and that same child would enter the waiting room. As they began their wait (under the guise they were waiting for the study to start), they were usually sitting down. But invariably they got up from their seats to undertake some male form of entertainment. They hung the child upside down until she giggled to death, messing up her hair and disheveling her clothes. They walked the room, exploring, or even wrestled on the floor until both were tired. Not one time did the dads sit passively, awaiting their appointments.

Not a single father quietly read a book. Not a single mother became a pro wrestler. Each parent fulfilled a need the child had that was unique to that parent's nature. Children become prepared for successful adulthood by growing up in an atmosphere of challenge and adventure from the father as well as comfort and caretaking from the mother.

Nurturing with No Regrets

In the question-and-answer section of your oral dissertation on the nature of a woman, ask your daughter this: When we live in a world of such need, why is it looked down upon that we women are nurturers by nature?

Every day you will encounter the helpless, the homeless, and those who are sick, hurt or injured. People are lonely; they need compassion, assistance, and love. We, women, have the unique ability to provide for much of this care. Make sure your daughter understands that nurturing is never a weak quality but a powerful one. When a woman recognizes a need and wants to help, she will move heaven and earth to make something happen. And when she does, the world changes!

A gender study has to include career choices as well—work both inside and outside of the home. The entire time my daughters were growing up, I had a career that kept me extraordinarily busy. My husband and I became self-employed three months after we were married and together built businesses our entire married life. I was never without, at the very least, a full-time job.

Evenings around the dinner table found our daughters often wearied by business discussions. They would beg, "Can we talk about something else?" We traveled a lot, taking them with us until formal education took precedence. When we lost control of their schedule, we committed to set parenting as our top priority. Often, we succeeded; sometimes, we failed. Our daughters knew this: they were our treasure over anything else God had given us, and our commitment to them was without surrender.

I loved our work and felt it was an essential part of who I was. It helped me to grow and do things I never knew I could accomplish. The example set for our daughters in my business life taught them that a woman could achieve anything.

But that example was not enough to help them become everything they could.

A personal clarifying moment came when some performers I was working with asked why I couldn't come to the airport to pick them up. They had flown in from a concert and needed a ride. I was having trouble working out their customary pickup and was about to surrender. Torn between my personal and corporate lives, I was overwhelmed by feelings of guilt.

Then my moment of clarity came. My response was this: "When I am old, and in the nursing home, I have only two people who may choose to visit me and wipe the drool from my chin. One is Chelsea, and the other is Loren. I'm going home."

And so, I did. All was not lost: the performers got a ride. I knew I had made the right decision. From that time on, I chose to arrange my business life around my daughters every time I could. To this day, I have no regrets. I was fortunate enough to have both—life with my family and accomplishment in our business.

When a woman recognizes a need and wants to help, she will move heaven and earth to make something happen. And when she does, the world changes!

But not all mothers work outside of their homes, and my keen appreciation of the roles of stay-at-home moms came to me shortly after we were married.

One of my husband's college friends and his wife had invited us to stay with them when we were traveling through the town in which they lived. I had never met either of them, so I was anxious to be liked.

We picked up my husband's friend at his office, where he rode with us to his home. Trying to make conversation, we talked about his family, his children...you know, small talk. Looking for a relatable platform, I asked the question often asked of a husband about his wife: "Does she work?"

His instant reply was this: "At the most difficult and important job in the world. She keeps our home and rears our children."

Boy, did I feel stupid, but he was right. We place so much value on jobs outside the home that we often forget one of our very most important roles—that of a mother. What could affect our world more than the molding of the generation that follows ours?

Our jobs in the home and outside the home—whether just one, a little of each, or a lot of both—are all places we find ourselves. Neither is the perfect or only solution. What's important is that you find yourself on the path uniquely created for you and that you don't judge those who are walking on different ones. I think we occasionally need to be reminded of the example set for us of the "noble wife" before we heap judgments on other women regarding their choices or wallow in guilt about our own.

The Proverbs 31 Woman

When seeking an example of a woman who successfully performed her duties, there is no better place to look than the last chapter of Proverbs. (And no, we're not looking at her to make you feel guilty.)

The writer described her at length as "a wife of noble character." This title makes me wonder who she was. (If you think the term *wife* is condescending, throw that idea out right now. That attitude comes from what is being taught in our University Gender Studies.) In today's world, we assume this title placed a limit on her position and abilities. After all, we pride ourselves on being so much more than "just a wife." So how can the life of this woman who lived so many years ago relate to any demands we as women encounter today?

Read the story yourself, and you'll realize nothing could be further from the truth. Yes, this woman was indeed a wife, but she was so much more.

Her husband seemed to like her a lot. In fact, the story says that, because of her, he looked good to his friends. But that wasn't all she was. She was kind and loving, a humanitarian, a landowner, a businesswoman, a mother, an employer, and a teacher. Take a look for yourself: the virtuous woman of Proverbs held every one of those positions! Now how is *that* for a job description? (Feeling exhausted yet?)

When we contemplate our overly committed, driven, obsessive women today, the Proverbs 31 woman had to have begun that parade. So, does this mean every one of us is supposed to be a teacher, landowner, businesswoman, wife, mother, and any other job someone can design for you? Well, no. Each mother is to apply the same premise of creative counseling to themselves that they have already to their daughters. You Mom should perform the duties and tasks that are unique to you, no more no less. Whether your life's work keeps you on the home front or at another workplace, rest assured that the Proverbs 31 woman could indeed be a description of you.

It was a few years ago that I had the pleasure of meeting another mom as we sat by one another on an airplane for a two-hour flight. As you do when confined to small spaces with hours to go, we began talking about our lives.

She was the mother of four grown daughters; I am the mother of two. She homeschooled her girls; I sent mine to public and private schools. She taught her daughters that since beauty was inside, that they shouldn't dye their hair or feel the need to wear makeup; I dyed my daughter's hair pink in elementary school and shopped with them at the cosmetics counters. She stayed at home each day caring for her girls; I left for the office juggling the workplace with the home front. After recounting our unique histories, we looked at each other and asked, "Well, how did it work out?" I am happy to report both of us replied, "Pretty good; we're proud of our girls." Then we went on to discuss their accomplishments. We had a wonderful conversation and enjoyed one another's company.

I am quite sure had we met when our girls were home in their growing up years; we would have probably asked the obligatory questions. She may have responded that she was a stay at home mom, and I would have replied I worked and traveled, raising my girls in the midst of my busy life. Then we both would have smiled, quickly pulling out our books and politely ignored each other as soon as we found out we had seemingly nothing in common. I feel confident we would have been afraid of the judgmental remarks that often follow when you state where you find yourself in life.

The conversation that goes something like this, "Oh you don't stay home with your daughters? I see. Don't you miss out on a lot? I'm sure you'll find you can't be there when your daughter needs you. Where will she turn if you aren't?" Or "Didn't you go to school to be anything more than *just* a mom? I would think just being a stay-at-home mom would be so unfulfilling. Are you really satisfied with that decision? And don't you want your girls to believe they can accomplish anything more in life than just housework and motherhood?"

The funny part is as we discussed our lives we both recounted those conversations. I was judged as the "working mom" by the stay-at-home moms. She was judged as the "stay-at-home" mom by the working moms. But now having grown daughters we know neither road is perfect, and neither road is always appropriate.

I wish I had known when my girls were growing up what I know now—we need each other, we need to support one another, and we must never judge. Walking off that plane, I reflected what different tracks she and I had taken and how amazing all six of our daughters were. Being a mom is hard enough without others telling you that you are doing it wrong. Remember: we only walk in our shoes…no one else's. So, forget those statements of judgment, get past the certainty that there is only one path, encourage one another in whatever shoes they fill, and remember this job can be done well in a multitude of ways.

Gender nature ≠ gender talents

There's one last thing I have to add to this doctoral study. Never confuse gender nature with gender talents. We are equal as men and women, but predictable we are not. Because you are a female, you aren't automatically a better cook. Because you are male doesn't enable you to fix the toilet.

When Christmas comes in our family, the Dewalt drill under the tree is tagged, Mom. I have received a drill, dremel, tool box, tool belt, and even a miter saw. These are gifts traditionally considered "men things." But I like fixing things. When we purchased our first home and had not one extra dollar for repairs, I figured out how to take a toilet down to the ground, fix all leaks, and put it back. We just could not afford a plumber, and I had the brain for the task.

My husband, on the other hand, was not blessed with mechanical reasoning. He stares at anything that needs repairing with a look of bewilderment. The talents given him are of the broad strokes: he is a visionary, a marketer. He has always been the one who dreams big and achieves goals other people don't think can be done. He is an information hound who makes well-reasoned decisions on everything from building a record company to marketing whatever project we are currently involved in and buying or selling just about anything. He leads the parade; I take care of the details. And this partnership has been the anchor of his and my lives through the best and worst of days.

So, Professor Mom, to complete that Professorship of Gender Studies degree, examine the cultural representation of gender offered to your daughters. Take the time to observe and study human nature to understand this subject. Resist the current thought that gender truth is something to be reinterpreted. Abandon gender identification as something that supersedes gender truth. It is belied by centuries of human history as well as the vast majority of science and medicine (which we will explore later in your job of Sex Ed Teacher).

But, most of all, embrace this—recognize your worth, your unique nature, and your distinct abilities. If we earn that doctorate for our betterment and then incorporate it into our lives, our daughters will most likely do the same.

Recognize your worth, your unique nature, and your distinct abilities.

If your daughter wants to take the Gender Studies class at her college of choice, make sure she has her head intact before she jumps in. She must fully understand a woman's and man's biology as well as the true nature of each. I can assure you those truths will run contrary to much of what is taught in that class. Sadly, if she disagrees with the teacher's academic premise, she may be treated only slightly better than the resident lab rats.

Since there is so much packed in this Gender Studies Professor job, here's a quick review.

› Women were legally denied equal rights, but that is no longer true. Statistics prove that we are afforded all of the opportunities we desire to pursue.

› Science proves that genders are indeed different. Life proves what those differences are and how delightful and complementary they can be.

› Our actions dictate our relationship with the opposite sex. Manipulating through sex has only a short-term effect; arguing and belittling tears a man down. If we respect and recognize the worth of a man's nature, more often than not, they will treasure ours.

› Finally, it is not where you work—whether inside the home, outside the home, or a little or a lot of both—that determines your success as a woman. It is embracing your nature as a woman and placing your priorities in what matters.

So now, Professor, begin the oral recitation to your audience—in this case, your daughter—and make sure you continue it until you no longer have breath.

The funny thing is, if you do, in a few short years you'll find her reciting the same things to *her* daughter…and someday to her daughter's daughter.

Now that's an enduring legacy of which you can be proud.

-7-

RELATIONSHIP COUNSELOR

| JOB DESCRIPTION |

Provider of counseling to develop the ability to recognize, avoid, manage, or reconcile troublesome differences in relational interaction. Through instruction, as well as information, instill within the counselee the knowledge needed to build and maintain a successful bond that ends in mutually enriched relationships.

YOUR DAUGHTER ARRIVES home from a date. She's beside herself when she comes to your room to tell you about it. "I'm in love," she says. "He's the cutest, sweetest, the most wonderful guy I've ever met." Her heart pounds when he's around. She loves to be seen with this young man. He makes her laugh, buys her presents, and says the most brilliant things. Etc., etc., etc., the accolades go on. Believable of any human they are not, but she thinks they are entirely true. In her eyes, this gentleman walks on water.

You, on this night, are fortunate, because she's reporting all of her crazy emotions to you.

The first time this scenario happens, she's a young teen. His name is penciled on notebook paper in never-ending doodles. The giggles are boundless when she's on the telephone with her friends and the terror upon seeing signs that he may like someone else is intense.

From your life perspective, you know this "love" is usually short-lived. This wonderful boy will lead to another terrific guy. She'll discover that he is not the love of her life and that he's not perfect, either. (It will take her even longer to discover that neither is she.) Indeed, something will change in that "amazing" relationship, and she will move on.

But if you tell your girl that fact in this moment of excitement, this "true love" might indeed last longer than you'd prefer it would just to prove you wrong. Keeping your mouth shut and numbly smiling is, without a doubt, your best defense. Remember: he is only *today's* Mr. Right. There are more to come.

Life predicts there will likely be a day when your daughter comes home with that look in her eye, telling you a certain someone is her one and only, the perfect man, *and on that day, she will mean it.* Maybe he's not a great guy. With your age and experience, you know things she doesn't. Human nature seen at twenty years old isn't as clear as that seen at forty years old. There's a good chance that you know the intent behind the flowers given and the sweet things said. You might also have the wisdom to realize that this young man will not be the faithful partner you'd want for your daughter. He doesn't possess what's needed to be half of a healthy relationship.

What should you do now? You are on dangerous and slippery terrain, and your responsibility as a mother is way behind the curve for these sorts of conversations. That's why it's so important that you *do not wait* until that day to instill the traits that make good and enduring life relationships.

The "Laundry List"

An effective Relationship Counselor spends years before that moment arrives helping your counselee know what a good man is and what it takes to build a healthy and reliable bond. The job has to begin early because when your daughter falls in love, she really FALLS in love. At this moment in your daughter's life, you can quickly become the enemy—the person who "understands nothing" and needs to be avoided at all cost. If she isn't looking for the right relationship before this moment, she can land squarely in love with the wrong one. Even if she is looking for it, he may be good at playing the part. And there's nothing you can do then to steer her away. But that shouldn't stop you from taking this job on, and the earlier, the better.

Early in my girl's lives, I created a laundry list for "the man they should marry." My relationship counseling began when my daughters were very young and thought boys had cooties. Then I repeated it to them when they entered middle school. Those were the days they liked a scrawny boy who was caught somewhere between Little League and cars.

My relationship counseling began when my daughters were very young and thought boys had cooties.

For the love-struck growing-up girl, the highs and lows swing wide. Your knowledge of her heartbreak might only come when you walk slowly by your daughter's bedroom door and stop to pick fuzz off the carpet. (In fact, it's such an unbelievable amount of fuzz that it takes quite some time to collect.) It's then that you "accidentally" overhear your daughter speaking to her best friend about her agony. Gaining knowledge, you can't let out that you know, you discreetly use that information in your ongoing counseling process.

High school was no different for my daughters. I again pulled out my Relationship Counselor card. Each time a boy came to the house

I nonchalantly mentioned my laundry list a short while later. The list was simple:

1. He pays his bills.

2. He loves his mother.

3. He loves God.

4. He loves you.

The list seemed silly to my daughters at the time. I got a lot of the rolling eyes, the "Oh Mom!" and the silence that said, "I am not listening." But there was a purpose behind the list I created.

Financial integrity

I had a method to my counseling madness. The character of the participants determines success or failure in relationships, and there are early indicators that will reveal that character. If a young man can pay his bills, he usually fulfills his commitments. There is a good chance integrity and honesty matter to him. If he can be forthright in his financial obligations, he will not carelessly get his family in debt, nor will he back down from his responsibility to his family.

Of course, such barometers are not foolproof, but they are great indicators for your daughter to gauge the integrity of the man she plans to spend the rest of her life with. I believe the instant gratification culture has created a great gulf in this character trait in both men and women. Many young men today have been raised to believe financial responsibility isn't important and not required, nor have they learned financial restraint. So, at the very least, if this young man is not good at the "don't spend more than you make" but great at everything else, then your daughter had better be good at it. And he must agree to hand the budget reins over willingly, leaving begging for possessions behind.

Financial integrity—the ability to keep one's financial commitments—is also one of the most obvious indicators on how capable a person is to keep all commitments. This includes the commitment to the very relationship your daughter is building.

Conduct toward his mother

A young woman should always look at how her boyfriend treats his mother. Relationship Counselors understand that his conduct toward his mother is an insight into his respect for and ability to love a woman.

Conversations between the young man and his mom are previews of the dialogues your daughter can expect to have with her spouse. He must be able to talk about both the important and the mundane. Females do both. But, if we women are honest, we'll admit we truly excel in the mundane. We can ramble on about *every* detail of *every* event. Most men hit the high spots and move on. They're good with that, even if it leaves us longing for more.

Finding a compromise between these opposing communication styles is, and will be, trying. Starting out on the right foot is crucial.

No relationship problem can be solved or, any understanding of issues reached unless a man makes the time to listen to what sounds to him like babble. At the same time, a woman must learn when she should simply shut up. That man can't and should not be expected to listen to every word spoken. (hint - leave the protracted version for your chats with your girl-friends who want you to tell all.)

If this boy can communicate with his mother concerning the important and the mundane, he's well ahead of the game.

If a son and mother love each other well, your daughter has a running start toward a rich, rewarding bond—not to mention the potential of a warm, mutual relationship with her mother-in-law, who is also then likely to treat her, as a new member of their family, with respect.

His love for God

As you and your daughter are considering the "spouse for life," concept, never forget that in every person there is a rooted faith. This even includes faith in the fact that there is no God on which to base your faith. This is the belief in something where there is no concrete proof. Believing there is no God isn't proven any more easily scientifically than the faith that there is a God. Sharing your root belief system is imperative to share a future. Finding a spouse who shares that faith is not only ideal but, a vital anchor to the potential success of a lifelong relationship.

Imagine spending the next fifty-plus years not talking about or acting upon your faith.

If consulting and relying on a spiritual authority is part of your daughter's decision-making process, it will be impossible for her to have a lifelong mate who doesn't feel that faith is vital to their daily life as a couple.

Imagine spending the next fifty-plus years not talking about or acting upon your faith. A couple shares a home, a car, a bed, and children but can't share their faith? It simply doesn't work. A Relationship Counselor must emphasize that sharing *all things* is crucial in a marriage bond—most of all, your faith. Why is this so important? Because our faith is the innermost part of our soul, and without sharing that depth, the marriage will never reach the richness this commitment intends.

His love for you

There's a reason I put financial integrity, his conduct toward his mother, and his love for God as the first three items on my laundry list, and I put "loves you" last. Most people believe "loves you" should be in the first position. But it's not the most important. (Right now, your jaw may have dropped. But hear me out first. Then you can decide for yourself if I'm off-base or not.)

Love is needed, desired, and a delightful element in all relationships. But love is currently viewed by our society as emotional, and emotion has great days and bad days. Its roller-coaster nature cannot be relied upon as a fix for the challenges that come as a result of daily life.

It's when love it becomes a verb—an action word—that it is most effective.

Love is truly wonderful and important, but as an emotion, it is not enough for success in building strong relationships. Love warms the heart, earns trust and confidence, and cares for others. But love's fickle nature can't be the only place to start a life. If it were, every boy—heart pounding and palms sweating—your daughter brought home would automatically attain the position of Spouse. (Now there's a scary thought, isn't it?)

No, instead it's when *love* becomes not a noun but a verb— an action word—that it is most effective. Love as an emotion is not enough, but love, when acted upon, becomes rich, rewarding, and successful.

Back to Basics: The Kindergarten Rules

There is another duty for the Relationship Counselor for creating the basis for success in relationships. This you will teach all throughout their lives, but the irony is that it comes from their early years. You see, kindergarten is the time to learn what makes every relationship successful.

Kindergarten Rules are great relationship counseling tools, and they include these:

> › Use an indoor voice.

> › Listen when others are speaking.

> › Treat others with kindness.

> › Be honest and truthful.

> › Share with your classmates.

Teaching your daughter these basic life rules and making sure she adheres to them is the foundation of any good relationship. If the Kindergarten rules are used at every stage in life, all relationships will be improved. But the marriage partnership will benefit the most.

A successful wife and husband are not "made" on the Wedding Day. In fact, that beautiful, exciting event that is all about them as a couple has no relevance on whether there even is a "them" twenty-five years later. What they have learned as the principal rules for the treatment of others is the cornerstone of all relationships, and this is especially true for their treatment of their future spouse.

Somewhere in my music business career, as I was walking down the office stairwell, I overheard guffawing, the excited comments, and the usual noise a group of tickled women can make. As I entered the conference room, I found these precious twenty-somethings eating lunch together. They were some of the brightest, most talented, fun, and delightful women you could ever meet. They worked extremely hard in every area and position of our business. We could not have succeeded without their efforts; they were the best of the best.

What had them so entertained? They had found an article supposedly from a 1950's home economics book. The publication was well before their years of education, and upon taking a peek I knew there was no way it would be part of the current education curriculum. Politically incorrect, this text would create a major uprising. But because I can't resist a good time, I joined the group.

What they were reading was intended for high school girls, to teach them how to prepare for married life.

What to Do When Your Husband Comes Home

› Have dinner ready: Plan ahead, even the night before, to have a delicious meal—on time. This is a way of letting him know that you have been thinking about him and are concerned about his needs. Most men are hungry when they come home, and the prospect of a good meal is part of the warm welcome needed.

› Prepare yourself: Take 15 minutes to rest so you will be refreshed when he arrives. Touch up your makeup, put a ribbon in your hair, and be fresh looking. He has just been with a lot of work-weary people. Be a little gay and a little more interesting. His boring day may need a lift.

› Clear away the clutter. Make one last trip through the house just before your husband arrives, gathering up schoolbooks, toys, paper, etc. Then run a dust cloth over the tables. Your husband will feel he has reached a haven of rest and order, and it will give you a lift too.

› Prepare the children: Take a few minutes to wash the children's hands and faces if they are small, comb their hair, and if necessary, change their clothes. They are little treasures, and he would like to see them playing the part.

› Minimize the noise: At the time of his arrival, eliminate all noise of washer, dryer, dishwasher, or vacuum. Try to encourage the children to be quiet. Greet him with a warm smile and be glad to see him.

› Some don'ts: Don't greet him with problems or complaints. Don't complain if he's late for dinner. Count this as minor compared with what he might have gone through that day.

› Make him comfortable: Have him lean back in a comfortable chair or suggest that he lie down in the bedroom. Have a cool or warm drink ready for him. Arrange his pillow and offer to take off his shoes. Speak in a low, soft, soothing, and pleasant voice. Allow him to relax and unwind.

› Listen to him: You may have a dozen things to tell him, but the moment of his arrival is not the time. Let him talk first.

› Make the evening his: Never complain if he does not take you out to dinner or other places of entertainment; instead try to understand his world of strain and pressure, his need to be home and relax.

› The goal: Try to make your home a place of peace and order where your husband can relax.

No wonder my colleagues were amused. This article contained the Stepford wife material—a view of a seemingly brainless, unimportant human created solely to fulfill her husband's needs. There also was no evidence that the counterpart instructions were written in any shop class textbook for the high school male student to prepare him for marriage.

So that day in the conference room we laughed in incredulity that any woman would be that crazy—or that "submissive"—to do those things.

Then, when the laughter died and, I walked away, it suddenly hit me as I headed up the stairs, back to my office: what if we women did just a *few* of those things for our men? Yes, times are different today. Many of us are in the workplace as well as keeping up with the home front. That means both parents arrive home tired from their day. Both need the quiet place of peace and order. But if we want that home, why don't we women step up and begin doing some little things that would go a long way in our man's heart?

I thought of the girls in the conference room. They were in various stages of relationships. It was a season when some had sworn off men after being hurt, others were in the casual dating phase, a few were in serious relationships or engaged, a couple had already married, and some were already divorced. To all of them, the list seemed absurd.

The next day I asked a few of them a question: What would happen if you chose only *two* of the things on the list to do or two like those. Then act upon them with a serious face!

Of course, some of the items on the 1950s list are unrealistic, but the premise behind the list isn't. I said, "Why not try it? And see what happens?"

I believed then and believe now that every woman would be amazed at how doing those two little things would affect how they were treated by the men in their life in return.

Why not take the challenge yourself? It isn't ridiculous to do something for your spouse to make his or her life better. It takes a strong woman, not a weak one, to commit to caring for another human for the rest of her life. And men today are so used to being treated as anything but special that they notice and love it when you show extra kindness and understanding.

And here's the reward for you: If your man is the kind who has the qualities for lasting relationship, and you chose him wisely, he'll do the same for you.

The Jewels in Your Treasure Box

Here's a lasting relationship tip: Kindness breeds kindness. It promotes emotional health. A relationship with two people caring for one another's needs takes the emotion of love to an entirely new level of action.

It's as if when you were first married, your love was that of a small diamond. Building a life together takes that treasure and, yearly add jewels. In the end, your love becomes more of a treasure chest than a single diamond. It is filled with all your "together" moments as you've faced financial struggle, financial success, your daughter's birth, and your daughter's rebellion. You've experienced the death of family members, cars breaking down, shopping for your first home, and loading the car for your daughter's first trip to college. Each of these life events, when experienced and handled together, adds another jewel to that chest of treasures that can never be taken from a committed couple.

My daughters cannot truly understand what over thirty years of marriage means to the depth of my husband's and my relationship because they have not experienced the length or depth of such a relationship yet. Nor can I understand the loss my father-in-law experienced when my mother-in-law died after forty-plus years of marriage. Half of who he is…was gone. A life partner is someone to be cared for and treated like a precious jewel. This is love in action. His or her worth is priceless. We need one another.

Your daughter desires a partner as well. Preparing her to be successful in this role is tantamount to her training.

In one episode of the old television program *Dr. Quinn, Medicine Woman,* a dialogue was going on between the shopkeeper and Dr. Quinn's youngest son. The two were lost in the woods together. The boy, then thirteen, was extremely confused and needed a man to discuss issues of his age. The issues, of course, were girls, sex, and how he should feel about the whole subject. Listening attentively, the shopkeeper pondered for a while before he made this statement: "A man needs a woman for one thing…." Of course, the show went to a commercial at that moment.

What is the one thing we all believe that men need women for? Sex, of course. I thought with dismay. *Surely the shopkeeper isn't going to be that simple. The writers have to do better than that.*

After awaiting the commercial break, the scene returned. The shop-keeper looked at the young boy and finished his statement: "...to believe in him."

I smiled. The writers certainly got that one right. A man can do anything if the woman he loves believes in him. A woman can do anything if the man she loves respects, cares for, and protects her.

Until death do us part?

I can't walk away from the subject of relationships without acknowledging where we find ourselves regarding the permanency of marriage: believing that marriage is intended to last until "death do us part"; that the promise made when you marry should never be treated lightly. The assurance you make to your future spouse on that wedding day should always be a promise you mean to keep. Current statistics tell us that nearly 50 percent of mar-riages in America will end in divorce.

So how do we maneuver through this new frontier? A great spouse and a fulfilling relationship is your hope, your dream for your girl, and for your own life. But I also know that you or your daughter may find you have entered an unexpected path. Choosing the wrong marriage partner can lead to anything but marital bliss.

Your daughter might have memorized that laundry list. She might be able to quote it to you backward and forwards. But the day may come when she inexplicably believes the list isn't relevant—at least not with *this* young man who is "close enough." Or she falls for someone who, on the surface, displays all of the character traits she is looking for...that is, until he becomes her spouse. You will probably see the truth before that time, but she doesn't.

Well, Mom, what do you do? Before she gets to that planned wedding day, when you know in your heart the relationship could be a mistake, you will discuss, cajole, and challenge, hoping to change her mind. You will lead them toward an effective premarital counselor to expose any future minefields. You will remind her of the list, look at the character of this future spouse, doing your best to get her off this course.

When you know in your heart the relationship could be a mistake, you will discuss, cajole, and challenge, hoping to change her mind.

But, sometimes, you just can't. This may be the one time she will not listen. Her heart is leading her decisions; her head is not. It is then you must love like you never have before, offering unlimited mercy and grace. She's got a rough road ahead.

If that happens, you must remain in her life and help her make this marriage work. Here's where you must have the grit (as well as the grace). Support this young couple. Listen and assist when you find tools that might make their marriage change course. Speak when you should; step out when you shouldn't. And above all, never give up hope.

But no matter what you or she does, the day may come when you receive that tearful call. The call to tell you she can't do it anymore and has determined to end the marriage (or her husband has). I can tell you this because I received that call and realized this was going to be my time of grace. My elder daughter needed me just like your daughter, if facing this, will need you. The pain she experiences as a result of her unwise decision will be heart-wrenching.

What I have learned about divorce is that it is a profound loss, one that creates grief, bereavement, and heartache, no matter what the cause. This is a loss of something that should have been, a loss of young dreams, heartfelt desires, and honorable intentions. You must love your daughter through the grief and the healing.

But it's not only your daughter who can face this challenge. You may find *yourself* as one of those "statistics"—a woman who is facing or has faced divorce. It's a situation you never thought you'd be in, and now you too must confront the same loss and disappointment. Mom, extend grace to yourself as well. Healing is offered and available to you in the same way it is your daughter. For the sake of your family and your future, you must embrace that healing and accept that grace, believing it is there for you. Without holding that in your heart, you won't be able to move forward in life with the grit that will be needed.

Mom, if you find yourself in that place of divorce, there's also one more difficult thing you need to do that your divorcing daughter may not. You must show grace toward the father of your girl. As her father, he holds a vital position in her life. She needs him, so it's incredibly important that you do your best to help her hold onto and build that relationship. Your words and actions will be one of the greatest determinants in achieving this goal.

Abigail Adams (the wife of John Adams, the second President of the United States) is a pure representation of the richness of marriage. This fascinating woman was strong, courageous, and often left alone while her husband followed his career path. While he was away, she successfully managed the family farm. During the Revolutionary War, she singlehandedly cared for their family while John defended the life he wanted for his country.

A man can do anything if the woman
he loves believes in him.

Their marriage lasted fifty-four years, yet many troubled days they were uncertain if they would both remain in this world. Life at these times was precarious at best since multiple people were out to kill the Patriot John Quincy Adams.

Abigail was known for her letters, spelling out the struggles through those trials. One such letter, dated October 16, 1774, and written just before the outbreak of war with Great Britain, told of her great relationship with John, her support and belief in what he did, and her emotional commitment to him:

> I dare not express to you at three hundred miles' distance, how ardently I long for your return.... And whether the end will be tragical Heaven only knows. You cannot be, I know, nor do I wish to see you, an inactive spectator; but if the sword be drawn, I bid adieu to all domestic felicity, and look forward to that country where there are neither wars nor rumors of war, in the firm belief that through the mercy of its King we shall both rejoice there together.

Your most affectionate
Abigail Adams

Knowing John was a man who had to fight for what he believed in, Abigail found herself in fear of his death. The real possibility of his demise lay heavy upon her heart. She feared her peaceful life would end, and she wouldn't regain happiness until they could once again meet in the "country where there are neither wars nor rumors of wars."

A woman can do anything if the man she loves respects, cares for, and protects her.

That kind of deep love and understanding between husband and wife is, what most only aspire to. Yet that is precisely the kind of love we need to teach our daughters to bring to this relationship and seek a partner willing to offer that kind of love as well. The Relationship Counseling pinnacle is an agreement made by both partners—an unselfish commitment to the betterment of the one they pledge their lives to. If you teach them that love is a verb when they are young, and they heed your instruction by seeking an equal partner with the same goals, it is a love that can be achieved.

-8-

SEX ED TEACHER

| JOB DESCRIPTION |

Provide direct instruction to students regarding human sexual anatomy, sexual reproduction, sexual intercourse, reproductive health, sexual identity, emotional relations, reproductive rights and responsibilities, and other aspects of human sexual behavior. Carry out a wide variety of tasks in the teaching-learning process for students—the primary one to help students learn the subject matter and gain the understanding that will contribute to their development as mature, able, and responsible adults.

D O WE HAVE to do this job? I mean, really? Undoubtedly, there are plenty of educational opportunities on human sexuality that are ready to instruct your daughter. They are abundant and come in the form of books, teachers, sex-ed classrooms, and don't forget television shows, the internet, movies, and even your daughter's friends. But it's this well-laid-out minefield of misinformation and agenda that makes it crucial this instruction is *yours* to give. The fact that the rest of the world is clamoring to meet this need pinpoints how vital this job is for a mom.

Is it easy? No, not when your goal is to provide clarity in the midst of competing views. Also, keep in mind that others who want to inform your child of the "facts" may have goals that often are not anywhere near yours.

Even the most open and forthright mom has issues with this job. After all, your sweet little girl is asking questions that require an enormous amount of frankness. You find yourself in a world that is delivering information to the public at large that is truly astounding as well as confusing. This leaves you with no other alternative but to be forthright even though you'd rather she forgets this subject for one more year to go back outside and play. *She's so young to talk about this,* you think.

But let me ask you: where else would you rather she go to get this kind of information? Can you think of a single better source than you, the one person who cares only about your daughter's well-being? You have no other motive but the best interest of your girl; indeed, you are the right person for this job.

You'd rather she forgets this subject for one more year and go back outside to play.

So, I made an early commitment to answer any question when asked—without hesitation or embarrassment, appropriately with complete honesty. There was nothing I would leave unanswered. Only ask, and I'd respond. I was determined to beat the other educators to the punch in a timely and well-thought-out approach.

It was a great plan, and it pretty much worked until the day my twelve-year-old daughter asked how the gay and lesbian communities had sex. I hadn't seen that one coming, and I swallowed hard. But then I stoically put on my game face. I asked her repeatedly if she was *entirely sure* she wanted to know. When she responded, "I wouldn't have asked if I didn't," with eyes rolling no less than four times, I inhaled deeply and jumped in.

To this day she still remembers that conversation well. And let me tell you, so do I. Her face mirrored every range of thought on this subject in her twelve-year-old mind. Her reactions were loud and, at times, humorous and priceless. I was working overtime to keep my expression impassively intact. The education was honest, factually correct, and without editorial. I'm not sure how well she slept that night, but she had just gained an education.

You may think that conversation is not appropriate to have with a child. Well, maybe it's not, but my daughter was curious about it. If I hadn't answered, she would have sought answers from someone else. I knew what I would teach her about this subject, but I didn't know what that someone else would say. Would she then have been educated with the truth, if she talked with someone who had an agenda to pass on?

This was the place I found myself in when my daughter was twelve. But today's conversations have taken on a whole new complexion. The information divulged in every arena of our culture will very likely require a mother to deliver education at a much younger age.

Sexual activities once limited to the gay community, those I found myself discussing with my daughter, are now being introduced to the heterosexual community as viable sexual experiences. Pornography, once considered a sinful indulgence hidden from your peers, is spoken of as a worthwhile exploration, a part of a healthy sexual experience. Same-sex attraction is not only a growing reality, but it is also very often encouraged among our thought leaders.

So, Mom, you are now a Sex Ed Teacher—whether you are comfortable with it or not. Don't let this frighten you! It is within your ability to do this. The good news is that while this job does require those "human sexuality" talks, a successful Sex Education comes from so much more than just biology.

By placing an enormous amount of importance on that one "birds-and-the-bees" conversation, we mothers miss the target. Many entities that feel sex education is their domain. Sexual education is not just taught in the school systems it is being shared in every form of life experience and entertainment in which your daughter participates. Television, Film, YouTube, social media and easily accessed internet sources have greatly expanded the means of past communication. The day your child can access the technological world, she doesn't even have to leave her bedroom to get the information she may be seeking.

Our entire community wants to educate our children on sexuality. Each entity prides themselves on their understanding of the issue. But if that education is so successful, why have we not changed the landscape of sexual confusion and consequence?

According to a recent CDC report[6] on teen sexual activity, 59% have had sexual intercourse, which is down from previous years. Of those surveyed, 30% had sex within the last three months, and only 49% of those used a condom. Half of the nearly 20 million new sexually transmitted disease (STD) cases reported *each year* are individuals between the ages of 15 and 24. In 2015, nearly 230,000 babies were born to teen girls age 15 to 19. The frequency of rape within the age group of 16 to 19 is four times higher than any other.

So perhaps neither public-school education nor organizations created for this purpose are "the solution." Even though the numbers for sexual activity did go down slightly, the potentially destructive consequences have risen. The ability to handle this issue does not come from any one educational program or influence. A girl must draw upon an entirely different platform to face the problems of sexuality—the confidence in her value and worth, embracing the belief that she was beautifully created and treasured by a perfect God who loves her dearly. It takes the love and nurturing of a family, intent on building that supportive belief system in every girl, to plant that seed of confidence.

Confidence in her self-worth is the only foundation that will enable a young lady to live in and get through a sexually drenched culture relatively unscathed. That means before being confronted with these issues; a girl must first believe in herself. A healthy, balanced view of herself *must* precede her knowledge of how others view her.

The Middle-School Years

The middle-school years are my least favorite years of life. They are the hardest, most emotionally agonizing times in the course of growing up. At least it seems that way when you are wading through it, both as mother and daughter. Having already made it through those years with my two girls I learned from first-hand experience, as well as some tough days, how that stage of life could begin to build up (or tear down) your daughter's self-worth.

It was a Tuesday afternoon that I received a telephone call from a dear friend of mine. She was on her way to the carpool line in front of her daughter's middle school, and she was distressed. I could hear the dismay in her voice and sense the angst in her heart. Her daughter was the product of the "mean girl" attack. We all know that one—girl against girl with the end purpose being, the superiority of one over the inferiority of the other.

Her precious, independent daughter was the object of the "you're weird, stupid, not cool, etc." attack. And it hurt. Worse, the daughter had just entered a new middle school and was seeking to find her place. She was being who she had always been and apparently, for certain middle-school peers, that wasn't acceptable.

For those of you who don't yet know, middle school isn't culturally about being you; it's about being like every other middle-school clone merely to fit in. The audacity of this girl to be an independent thinker was repugnant to the middle-school elite. And the daggers of ridicule rained upon this sweet child.

I believe it hurt my friend, like most of us mothers, as much or more than it injured her daughter. What to do? Call the teacher, the other girl's parent, fight back, kick the girl in the car pool line, ignore her, or something else? This was the debate. Have you ever seen a lion cub defended by its mother? In this scenario, a mother can make a lioness look lightweight.

Middle school isn't culturally about being you; it's about being like every other middle-school clone merely to fit in.

When my daughters were subjected to this challenging rite of passage, my creative imagination was brilliant, if I do say so myself. Picture the scene with me:

I, the mother, comes to the defense of my bullied daughter. Wheeling into the school parking lot, horn blazing, tires squealing, I stop traffic and leap out of my SUV to confront the mean girl who is making my daughter miserable. Everyone stands aside, stricken into silence, as I stride forward until I am toe-to-toe with Middle School Diva. What do I tell her?

"Back off! If you even as much as look at my daughter the wrong way, you will deal with me. And by the way, if you don't know, 'Miss Smug Little Think I'm All That,' you are a blip on the screen of humanity. The only place in life you will feel important is here and now, and trust me, it will soon be gone."

The crowd around me, evidently as sick of Miss Diva as I am, cheers and applauds. My daughter looks at me in awe as her hero.

I load up the car and head home, problem solved....

Okay, so I didn't do it. It wouldn't have worked. My daughter would have been mortified, dying of embarrassment instead of bullying.

But I must say that dreaming it at the time felt good...*incredibly good*. When I calmed down, I realized these were the insane fantasies of an out-of-control lioness defending her cub. My basic instinct was to protect, fight, and make the wrong right. But what was needed was my ability to maintain reason and sanity...and then do what was best for my daughters.

Girls need to understand that middle school (and even sometimes in elementary) is only the *beginning* of a series of these conflicts. Throughout her years on this earth, your daughter will encounter people who feel the need to rebalance the playing field of life. They will be requesting things of your daughter that are not in her best interest. These people will do their best to manipulate their point of view into the mind of your girl. That's because they must feel superior to, advance beyond, and even sometimes have the apparent need to be mean to the people around them. Sad to say, many of these individuals don't outgrow the middle school scene; they practice it in daily life even as adults.

So, this is the perfect opportunity to teach your daughter practical self-worth. My friend's girl had been reared to be an independent thinker—to follow her unique path based upon a specific value system. She had a healthy dose of self-worth already instilled. Did that mean the bullying didn't hurt? Of course not. But the nurturing given by her parents during her first twelve years was now faced with a life test.

This is the moment for practical Sex Education—not the "sex talk" but the "how to live independently among those who want to bring you and your gender down" talk.

I said to my troubled friend, "Tell your daughter this—life is full of people who have different opinions than yours. A lot of them will be uncomfortable with the fact that you won't agree. Instead of accepting an independent thinker, they choose to attack, thinking they can cause you to relent and become 'one of the pack.' These people find it unacceptable that a confident free thinker stands unaffected in their midst. They need to feel important, and in charge, so the verbal assault you're getting is to make them feel superior. They must make others conform to their attitudes to create their self-importance."

"A child who doesn't follow the path of these personalities is an obstacle to them. If you are simply yourself, hold to what you believe, and feel good about who you are, they have nowhere to go and nothing left to ridicule. They have lost their effectiveness. That will be the one thing that truly drives these girls out of their minds."

This is one of the essential life lessons your daughter needs to learn early and well. It doesn't mean your daughter, as the recipient of the attack, won't feel hurt or alone; she will. But if your daughter learns in middle school that the basis of the attacks is the attacker's need or desire rather than your daughter's inadequacy, she'll be way down the road in dealing with other life pressures. She'll be able to face opponents with a different attitude, an understanding of why it's happening, and her self-worth will stay intact.

Attacks are based upon the attacker's need or desire, rather than your daughter's inadequacy.

So, Mom, don't do anything rash or take things into your own hands, in your current middle-school crisis…at least not yet. First, talk to your daughter; remind her how special and unique she is. Educate her so she understands this form of confrontation. Let your daughter know that this is the beginning of people trying to influence her actions. As long as she embraces her independent personality to make her own decisions, these people will come in and out of her life, with limited effect. She will learn that she is capable of not allowing them to control or manipulate her to be someone she is not.

The one thing you must do as a communicator is to make sure your girl is talking. If she is sharing such struggles with you, she'll be alright because you can lend perspective and also keep a keen eye on the situation. Indeed, if it gets worse, and you are seeing it take a permanent toll on your child's self-worth, you must find a way to intervene. But don't jump in if they are just dealing with the fallout. It's permanent damage that you work to avoid. Know that hurt and recovery create strength. So, if your daughter can get through this situation with her independence and self-worth intact, she has passed a crucial test for the challenges that lie ahead.

Putting Sex in Its Place

Right now, you might be wondering, *Sounds like good advice, but what does all that have to do with sex?*

Self-worth has absolutely everything to do with it. Sex is powerful and one of the most manipulated subjects in our culture. Simplified, every boy is a walking hormone; every girl innately understands the power of sex.

At seven years of age a little girl giggles and flirts; then a little boy chases her and pulls her ponytail. In unison, they both yell at each other, "Cooties!" This is the elementary school mating dance. Middle school is full of confused relationships; high school begins the courtship in earnest.

Every boy is a walking hormone; every girl innately understands the power of sex.

A girl must believe that she is created for much more than the physical gratification of someone else. That knowledge will temper the influence of sexual pressure upon her life.

I often wonder where we got the idea that our children have no self-control. We speak of them as if they are no more than animals in mating season. We act as if they are unable *not* to have sex, so we've lowered our expectations: "When you're ready and with the right person, practice safe sex," the discourse goes. But what are we saying? Early and uncontrollable sex is a given for our daughters, so try to do better? Nowhere in the majority of sexual education is the "Hey, it might be a great idea *not* to have sex" plan.

No disease, no unwanted pregnancy, no lowering of self-esteem, and no regrets are a few of the many benefits of abstinence. As in all other aspects of life, do we not want the absolute best for our daughters?

Modern sex education tries to convince us that times have changed, and there are no consequences to the change in attitude toward the sexual experience. The facts don't bear that out, as shown by a survey of teens ages 15-17 done by the Kaiser Foundation in partnership with *Seventeen* magazine[7]. These findings reveal that 76 percent of girls and 55 percent of boys regretted having sex. In a second survey done by *Seventeen* magazine and the Ms. Foundation, a thousand 13 to 21-year-olds were surveyed; 81 percent of the girls and 60 percent of the boys regretted the decision to become sexually active. Interestingly, these studies were not done by an organization that actively promotes abstinence.

In gleaning more data from the CDC study, we find not only does the young population have the highest rate of STD's, but they also receive the most physical damage from them. Two in five teen girls who have contracted an STD discover theirs can cause infertility or even death. The human papilloma virus (HPV) is an STD that causes genital warts and is also the cause of 90 percent of diagnosed cervical cancer in later years. HPV is also the current number one cause of oral cancer. The acceptance of casual oral sex has created an outbreak that has outpaced smoking in causing this horrific and deadly illness.

Stunningly, all STDs are sexist; they statistically do more severe physical damage to women than men. In other words, it's our girls who will be hurt the most. A readily offered answer to this problem is the HPV vaccine. Recently, mothers have questioned both the efficacy and side effects of all vaccines offered to their children. Mothers research the early vaccination schedule, hoping to make right decisions; even the flu vaccine requires a second look. So, without sufficient history and studies on the side effects of the apparent answer to HPV, reticence to allow that to be given to your teen girl seems a reasonable and wise stance to take.

It's not just physical but also emotional damage that can occur. The rate of depression among teenage girls having sex is 25.3[8] percent while the rate among teens not having sex is only 7.7 percent. The percentage of attempted suicides among sexually active girls is 14.3 percent compared to the 5.1 percent who maintain abstinence. If the best interest of our girls is our sole motivation we cannot ignore the stats.

One of the newest attitudes among the thought leaders on this subject is their desire to blur the lines of sexual identity, encouraging parents to have a gender-neutral disposition. Even to believe it may be in the best interest of their child to consider altering the sex of one who finds himself/herself in the "wrong body."

In May of 2017, the *American College of Pediatricians*[9] addressed this new phenomenon. The article opened with this sentence, *"The American College of Pediatricians urges healthcare professionals, educators, and legislators to reject all policies that condition children to accept as normal, a life of chemical and surgical impersonation of the opposite sex. Facts – not ideology – determine reality."* An incredibly bold statement, don't you think? Especially in light of the ongoing dialogue urging us to accept the fluidity of gender identity.

The publication went on to discuss the often real and very normal confusion of children as they enter puberty. *"Puberty is not a disease, and puberty-blocking hormones can be dangerous. Reversible or not, puberty-blocking hormones induce a state of disease—the absence of puberty—and inhibit growth and fertility in a previously biologically healthy child. According to the DSM-V, (Diagnostic and Statistical Manual of American Psychiatric Association) as many as 98% of gender-confused boys and 88% of gender-confused girls eventually accept their biological sex after naturally passing through puberty."*

With these facts, why are we viewed as out of touch to believe boys are boys and girls are girls? Confusion as part of the transition is common through puberty. Additionally, why would we not encourage abstinence as the best choice for our girls? Protecting your child from regret, depression, emotional issues, and physical problems, including cancer that can lead to death, seems a no-brainer—the right thing to do.

Understanding that the lessons taught may be lost in a moment of pressure or emotion, it is still a job we need to take. Realizing others are contradicting our beliefs should not deter us. It would seem a teacher on any subject would want to teach principles of success. So why should Sex Ed be any different?

But in this job as Sex Ed Teacher, we have to understand that our girls will make their own choices. When they make ones you wish they hadn't, in this difficult and challenging arena, you will be there to walk alongside, in the same way you were when you began this conversation.

While you are educating on this subject, you cannot avoid explaining the pleasure of sex as well. *What?* You're saying. *Why would I do that?*

First, if we act as if sex cannot be fun, we are not truthful. To many mothers, it may seem that downplaying the sexual enjoyment will dissuade your daughter from having sex, so taking away the upside to the subject appears to be a decent plan. Well, it's not. Physical pleasure can be found in any healthy sexual relationship. If you are honest in your education, which must be your commitment (otherwise your daughter will go to other sources for the information), you must give the complete, unabridged version.

"Sex can be fun anytime—pushing the right buttons, brings physical pleasure," you tell your daughter. "But it is only fully and completely pleasurable, emotionally and physically, and without damaging side effects in the marriage relationship with your life partner." Yes, I did say in the marriage relationship, let me unpack that.

In today's culture where one segment of society is fighting for the right to marry, and the other is often choosing not to, one must ask oneself why the disparity? I believe it's both the significance as well as the disillusionment of the institution. There is an innate understanding that the state of marriage brings a higher level of commitment. Thus, the push in one segment of society. While there is also an understanding that marriage so often fails, which brings many couples to the place that living together becomes a reasonable option.

But marriage is different than living together. It is a stronger commitment that is more difficult to dissolve, harder to walk away from. It requires a legal contract in the form of a marriage license between two individuals.

Living together, while on the increase, does not appear to be the answer to maintaining a long-term relationship. Statistics show those who cohabit before marriage have a nearly 50% higher divorce rate than those who don't. There is a difference between beginning a relationship with the intention of marriage, even if choosing to cohabitate first and those who merely slide into the marriage. Relationship security, or lack of, always hinges on a real commitment.

While correct that a marriage license is just a piece of paper filed at the local county clerk's office, it is what that piece of paper represents, and what the signatories agree to, that is significant. A commitment to one another that is not easily or quickly dissolved, a willingness to sign your name with the intention that the only thing that will divide is "death do us part." No other agreement, spoken or written, that has the same impact or holds the same promise.

Controlling Sex...Before It Controls You

The most-wise man who ever lived was King Solomon. Though known for his wealth, his proverbs had a lot to say about relationships. It is astounding to me that a man who married 700 women and had 300 concubines was considered the wisest man who ever lived. Having a gaggle of women under one roof, with you as the only man, isn't the most brilliant thing Solomon ever did. In fact, it seems like lunacy! But it does appear that early in the king's life he understood the depth and commitment of love. He wrote of love, passion, and sexuality in the Song of Songs—a book about a relationship between a man and woman.

This story is a narrative from the lover, beloved, and friends of the lovers. It is a beautiful portrait of what a love commitment should be. The lover and beloved are entering marriage having waited for each other sexually and now will share their lives in every way. There is one statement repeated by the object of his love, his wife to be, the beloved. In speaking to fellow maidens about her passion for this man she shares wise instruction with her peers: "Do not arouse or awaken love before it so desires."

Understanding that there is a time to arouse and awaken love, she warns that prematurely doing so serves an injustice to a future relationship of sharing and commitment. The natural act of love is sex. But remember that *love* and *sex* are not automatically synonymous. They are and always will be *separate acts* most perfectly entwined with our life partner.

In a culture that creates the impression that we as humans are slaves to the power of sex, how do you not arouse love? How do you not take that next step? The current thought is we are incapable of controlling sex; it controls us. So, do we believe the theory that teens are incapable of keeping their pants zipped, so just make sure they have protection? No, young women can choose to stay out of the back seat. But they must understand the practical side of how to do so.

For years, my daughters' lullaby was Stevie Wonder's "Isn't She Lovely?". Our love song to our girls. It's still a very treasured song in our family. But when they became older, I added a new song to the family musical repertoire. "(Don't you) Feel My Leg" was a song performed by Maria Muldaur when I was in my late teen years. It's a very useful tool in the education you are trying to achieve. The lyrics go like this:

> Don't you feel my leg, don't you feel my leg cause when you feel
> my leg you're going to feel my thigh and if you feel my thigh you're
> going to tell a lie so don't you feel my leg.

Don't you drink that wine, don't you drink that wine, cause when you drink that wine you'll try and change my mind, and if you change my mind you'll feel my fine behind, so don't you feel my leg.

You said you'd take me out like a gentleman—treat me fine, though I know that's just something at the back of your mind. If you keep drinking oh you're going to get fresh, and you'll wind up begging for this fine, fine flesh.

Don't you feel my leg, don't you feel my leg cause when you feel my leg your gonna feel my thigh, and if you feel my thigh you gonna go up high, so don't you feel my leg.[10]

No, it isn't a sweet lullaby, but it's practical and full of truth, isn't it? Be willing to set Sweet Mommy aside when you tackle this job of Sex Ed. Use whatever tool necessary, including the magnificent ditty I just shared with you. Any mother who thinks she must be delicate about this subject is fooling herself.

It is also true that a girl doesn't wake up one morning and say to herself, *I think I'll have sex today.* Like everything else, this happens gradually. Kisses lead to cuddling, which leads to hands, which leads to clothing unbuttoning, which leads to oral sex, which then ends up as ultimately full-on, no-stopping-the-train sex. And we all know this doesn't happen in one night.

A girl doesn't wake up one morning and say to herself, I think I'll have sex today.

Instruct your daughters that each act leads to another act. It is not on a date that decisions are made not to have sex; it is at home-*before* the boyfriends, the dating, the automobile rides, the dances, or any other teen experience.

In Sex Ed your daughter will receive the sex talk, the biology version that begins with scientific facts, to the "don't do it" line, and that talk will end with "see you in a few years." But don't stop there; educate your girl to understand action and reaction from her and the boy...*any* boy. Prepare her, train her, and teach her. Use whatever example or phrase is needed to paint the picture for your girl. Expect the rolling of the eyes, but don't let that stop you.

› If there's no gas in the car, it won't run. (A classic line my daughters thought was stupid.)

› He won't buy the cow if the milk is for free. (This was the truth spoken by Minnie Mom.)

› "Don't you feel my leg cause..." (Make sure they know the rest of the song.)

Get Creative

A dear friend of mine had a creative approach when her daughter once purchased her bikini made up of a few well-placed hearts. My friend told her daughter it was inappropriate, bringing attention where she really shouldn't have it. This attention would only create problems for her and any boy who wasn't blind. She got the "Mom; you're wrong! It does not, and you don't understand. And I'm not taking it back either!" response as her daughter stomped away into her room and slammed the door.

Frustrated with her seeming inability to get across truth to her daughter, this creative mother tried another approach.

The family always had pets, and this year they had a cute, little house dog. Taking scissors, construction paper, and tape the mother went to work. Cutting out three hearts and creating two-sided tape she stuck the hearts on the belly side of the dog in the same places they would be on her daughter.

Then she called her family into the room. Holding the front paws of the dog up, with the hearts dominating the scene, she paraded the dog around the room on his back feet while singing an old 60's tune, "Itsy Bitsy Teeny

Weeny Yellow Polka Dot Bikini." After the family got off the floor from laughing, they revisited the conversation.

"Where exactly did you look when you first saw the dog?" the mom asked.

There was no denial, but an admission that eyes were drawn elsewhere; not to the cute little snout or puppy dog eyes. Her girl couldn't argue with that. The mom's point was made and accepted; the suit returned to the store. So why not be original in your presentation? Who needs another lecture? Get creative!

Sexuality is powerful, and girls know it. Saying that again, girls know it. When a girl dresses provocatively, and unnecessary skin revealed boys' heads turn. That's the simple part to figure out. The challenge is interpreting what is "too much skin." Doing so is an essential role for us mothers as we battle the sexual behavior frontier.

Appearance matters to most girls. They want to wear the stylish clothes, be cute, and fit in, and inevitably this creates the forever divide between generations. Can they have uniquely dyed hair (probably), facial piercing (maybe), short skirts (well, define "short")? Styles are determined by your daughter in many ways. You have to help her find the one that enables her to feel good about herself, while at the same time not presenting herself as a person willing to do something she doesn't want to do.

Finally, as you determine your Sex Ed strategy, I have four suggestions.

#1: When addressing modesty, don't engage.

During my clothing struggle years with my daughters, a wise woman gave me great advice. When your daughter reaches thirteen, she's in the dressing room, and she says, "Mom, what do you think?" you never—I mean *never*—give the straight answer. Saying, "You are crazy if you think you're going out in public, let alone out of this dressing room, wearing that! That's gonna happen over my dead body," isn't exactly the recipe for success.

Instead, being the wise mother, you have become, your response should always be, "I'm not sure, honey. What do you think?"

Then she will respond with her uncertain comments since at that age they are almost always unsure about everything. Quickly you have your exit strategy from a potential catastrophe. Acknowledge her doubt and create a discussion about color, print, or any innocuous, non-threatening aspect of her garment. Leading the conversation where you be able to say, "You are so pretty! We have to find something that makes you shine. This just isn't good enough."

Your response should always be
"I'm not sure, honey. What do you think?"

This type of conversation is so much better than the alternative one that ends with the defiant, "Mom didn't like it, so I'm buying it and wearing it to church!"

Without a doubt, this technique works. I've used it a million times myself with both my daughters—and avoided at least that many quarrels. When not in the middle of a department store struggle, a mother should find time for further conversation where there are no other potential emotional bombs ready to go off. As you're in the car singing oldies together, or watching TV, comment on some cute but fashionable outfit that you think would look great on your girl. Believe me; she'll pick up on it.

#2: Wage war on what matters long-term.

Your daughter needs to know that in every part of life, half of a battle is won before she ever gets to war. In business, when the one with whom you are negotiating thinks you are a great negotiator, you will get a better deal before you even start the process. In entertainment, if you look like a celebrity, you are perceived as one well before success enters your life. In the real battlefield of war, if you look like the stronger army, the enemy thinks they have a good chance of losing, so hesitancy on their part leads to your victory.

It is the same in sexuality. When a girl is dressed like she's ready to play, she'll be asked to play. The best way to avoid that assumption on the part of the boy is not to look like you think you were made for his entertainment. Now, I'm not talking turtlenecks and corduroy pants that are a size too big; I'm talking about practical compromises. Never forget your daughter has to survive in the teen culture, so let style be incorporated into her world. For example, the day my daughter wanted pink hair, I didn't have a problem with it. It wasn't a battle that mattered. However, neckline to belly button *is* the war that needs to be waged.

Protect them, prepare them, support them, believe in them, and choose your battles: this is all part of effective sex education. Our daughters do not have to fall slave to current philosophies.

When it comes to sex, "the first time" philosophy comes to our girls defined in many ways. What is the appropriate first time? When you're in love, he's amazingly cute, or the full moon is out? Clarity on this position requires definition on the part of the mother.

I look back to when my daughter took her first airplane trip by herself, to visit her grandparents on her own when she was eight years of age. She spent part of her homecoming day with me at my office. She loved wandering around our staff desks and talking to the wonderful people who worked for us. That day I got distracted with work and lost her in the building.

While rounding a corner as I searched for her, I heard her going from desk to desk, proudly telling people she took her first airplane trip all by herself. I stayed hidden as I listened to the responses that inevitably included stories of each person's first plane-ride memory. It struck me that day that a first in life only happens once. It can't be rewound and done again. Then it's over and is a memory.

So, find your own story, your example to teach your daughter that there is only one first.

A first in life only happens once.
It can't be rewound and done again.

With sex, that first memory should always be a treasured one. Because of our culture's standards, often it is not. It is still best if your girl defines that "first" with the man she has committed to spending the rest of her life with. Although today this feels like an ideal, an unrealistic dream, we must remember that such an experience will forever make that "first time" special. Should she make this choice, the day will come without regrets, bringing no other past relationships into that moment, and will allow them to experience the wonder of sex in the most precious, fulfilling way.

#3: Reinforce her worth.

Every daughter should know that no girl born was created to be the object of another's sexual gratification. She was not brought into this world to be viewed as merely a sexual partner.

Take every opportunity to remind her of what you taught her from the time she was young. She is a treasure and should expect anyone who says they care for her to treat her as such. She should also understand that any boy she gets involved with has worth as well. As shown in Kaiser's study, boys can have regrets, too. The emotional and physical impact of sexual activity is not just felt by your daughter.

Find an opportunity to ask simple questions that make her ponder. You may discover the best time to start this dialogue is apart from an intense conversation about sex. Questions like these, "Do you think I would ever ask you to do something that may cause you physical harm?" "What would you do if something was said to you that made you uncomfortable, whether it came from a guy your age or an adult?" "Would your best friend try to talk you into doing something that everything in you didn't want to do?" "Would you remain friends with them if they brought it up time and time again until you finally gave in even if they knew you didn't want to?" Create other innocuous analogies and ask thought-provoking questions. Your goal is to make her understand what real love is.

These kinds of questions give you the opportunity to create a discussion away from a concerning relationship. Your goal is for her to realize if the boy she cares about is asking these things of her it is not for her desires. These requests are being made for his.

Finally, it has been proven time and again that a female cannot have casual sex without an emotional commitment, a man can. Not only is she risking the possibility of health problems, or pregnancy when she isn't ready for it, but she's also headed for a broken heart. Make sure she remembers she is worth more than that.

#4: Realize you will both make mistakes.

Now, Mom, I can't end this chapter without making you keenly aware of something I learned through life experience. You will, at times make mistakes in this career of motherhood. Know that your daughter will also make mistakes too, and sex leads the way during the teen and young-adult years. The subject of sex brings the greatest amount of confusion, conflict, and pressure to your daughter.

Don't be surprised if your daughter steps over lines she never meant to. There is, in fact, a good chance she will. But your role as Sex Ed Teacher doesn't end if your daughter steps past holding hands and kissing into more dangerous territory. It doesn't stop if she becomes sexually active.

If any of those challenges are in your life right now, make sure you have lived in a way that demonstrates an enormous amount of grace. Show grace to other moms, other daughters, friends, and family members who are dealing with consequences of choices in this arena filled with minefields.

If you have shown that grace, and the day comes when your daughter has her own compromises to deal with, there is a chance she will believe she will receive the same. She will share her struggles with you and ask for your advice. Your relationship as, mom and daughter will go on, forging a stronger-than-ever bond. Perhaps she now realizes that, in at least this area, your words were right, even though you don't remind her.

Has she disappointed you? Yes. Are you wondering what you did wrong? Yes. Do you wish you could rewind life's clock? Absolutely, yes! But you can't, and your daughter needs you now more than ever. What she is currently walking through is not abstract but concrete with real-life consequences.

Don't be surprised if your daughter steps
over lines she never meant to.

She may have guilt, confusion, and regrets, have an STD or even have become pregnant. She may be dealing with same-sex attraction or have chosen not to marry the man she loves but to live with him. Don't let her down now. Sex Ed Teacher, your job is even more crucial in these moments. The support you give her, the grace you extend to her and the insights you can provide are more important than ever before. The honest conversation you had committed to can't end here. The most important thing you can show her now is the depth of her place in your heart. She may have lost her way, but you can make sure she doesn't lose you.

Mom, love your daughter now in the same way you loved her the first day you met. Remember that day? You knew then there would be no mountain too high, no river too wide, no battle too great. Can you listen when she says things you don't want to hear? Can you reach out to the man she's living with extending the love you have for her? Can you help her forge a road on which you never wanted to be? Did you mean what you said and thought that day she was born? I bet you did. And now's the time she'll know you did.

FINANCIAL CONSULTANT

| JOB DESCRIPTION |

Supply financial solutions to client, educating them on means of improvement of their financial decisions. Provide the assistance needed to meet financial goals through personalized, in-depth counseling and recommendations of appropriate money management.

THERE WERE YEARS as my girls were growing up that I was the "end cap" queen of America. For those of you who don't know, an end cap is the shelf space at the end of each aisle in almost every store in our nation. It's the "this is an unbelievable deal" vortex that pulls in busy women when they are shopping in a hurry. It's the place where retailers place the coolest stuff at the best prices. Really, can these buys be resisted? Not by me, at least for a time in my life. I mean, can we live without a portable chopper that works off batteries, cutting everything instantly into the appropriate-sized pieces? But get it home and find out what a nightmare it is to clean after shredding all of your food instead of that promised "clean chop."

Or the cute little top that was only $6.99…and still lies at the bottom of your drawer. (It doesn't match a thing you own.)

Seeking one lost shoe on the floor of my daughter's closet would require weeding through the pile of must-have toys or undone projects purchased on a whim.

In hindsight, I wonder how much money I've spent on "stuff." I don't think I want to know; it would probably make me ill. Back then I was vulnerable, in a hurry, drawn into the eddy of great deals. My jobs kept me running while taking care of my family, our home, and our dog. I was merely trying to stay afloat without sinking. I was the perfect mark for retailers.

I don't say this to excuse my bad habits; what I did still wasn't brilliant financial planning. But I fell into mindless spending…until it occurred to me that these stores were winning the game. Even more, than them beating me at the retailopoly they played, I realized my actions served as my most effective teacher, and I was instructing my daughters every time I grabbed an item off the store shelf. What were my daughters learning from me? That a quick, mindless purchase was okay.

One of my jobs as Mom was to teach financial responsibility, and I wasn't practicing it. So how could I expect them to?

The Financial Consultant's job is to understand money, to know what importance it holds, and how to manage it. Mom, this job begins in *your own* life. You don't have to be an accountant to do this well. Just know how much you earn, don't spend more than you make, and don't purchase things you don't need. Never waste what you've worked so hard to earn.

If you are expecting schools to teach this to your child, dream on. Remember from your Academic Advocate position that they care about algebra and calculus, not consumer math. The job is yours: to help your daughter learn how to survive financially in this money-driven culture. It's okay if math is not your thing; what you need to teach are financial limits and a balanced, healthy perspective.

The Allure of Money and Things

I have been bewildered at the broadly held belief that money holds answers and eliminates all life problems. How many times have we heard, or even said, "If I could only win the lottery." A million or a hundred million seems as if it would solve a whole lot of problems, especially when you sit down to pay your monthly bills. Of course, a big chunk of change, (for that matter, an even smaller one) could eliminate that life pressure. But what money doesn't do is remove all hurt, solve life conflicts, and guarantee happiness.

While waiting for an elevator in LA with my daughter, who was on her way to see a doctor, we were joined by an apparently wealthy and extremely elderly fragile woman. She was in a wheelchair pushed by a private nurse. Dressed impeccably, with a vast number of valuable jewels on her hands and around her neck, she appeared unbelievably frail. But as she barked unkind orders to her nurse, we realized she was unhappy with everything around her.

As she boarded the elevator with us, I could only think, *Well, her wealth certainly didn't put a smile on this lady's face.* She was obviously very ill, toward the end of her life, miserable, and accompanied by a nurse, instead of a loved one. She was a living example of wealth not bringing with it all that matters.

The "I wants."

Don't think your daughter is safe from the deceptive allure of things. The "I want" attitude permeates the world around us; with the importance of possessions taught at a very early age. The first time you turn on the television to view a children's program she is inundated with commercials that sell her the best new toy. Even the program itself has spun off a whole selection of merchandise. What she sees on the screen lines the toy aisles of the stores you visit. A mother has to try her very best to steer clear of these quite colorful and enticing displays found in nearly every retail establishment you frequent.

All through her life, she will discover a new "got to have" item. Whether it is toys, cereal, shoes, makeup, new fashions, a computer, a new app, or the latest cell phone, these alluring items come fast and hard at your daughter every day. Each product is inescapably linked to happiness, beauty, and life fulfillment!

If you don't get drawn into this black hole of buying the latest and greatest, you will indeed help your daughter avoid it. Now I'm not saying each, and every purchase is wrong or that we should all live communally without possessions. I lived that way for a while and, trust me; it has its pitfalls. What I am telling you is that you must have a *reason* to make purchases.

The "I want" attitude
permeates the world around us.

When I transitioned from end-cap mania to control over my purchases, I began a new philosophy of spur-of-the-moment buying for my daughters. Instead of buying everything offered, we started the tradition of purchasing a purposeful, not holiday-related gift. Occasionally I would buy what we called an "I love you" present; special items not based on a day or event. Not buying because someone in the shopping cart was whining over the "must have" they spotted, or because I couldn't walk by the most amazing, well-priced item on the end cap.

These purchases were made because I loved my daughters. I wanted to show them a simple, non-pressured way to receive gifts. I did this occasionally, not every time we entered a store. And when I did, it was a special gift at a particular moment for no reason other than I loved them. That was a great reason to make a purchase. They and I treasured those gifts more than any related to a life event.

Money—evil or good?

You will find there is another view held by many while you are training your daughters (as well as yourself) to spend money appropriately. This outlook is interchangeable and dogmatic, depending upon the financial position you're viewing it from.

The first is that money is evil, and those who have it did something wrong to get it. This view normally comes from one who doesn't have it.

Others think that possessing money proves worth and importance. This thought comes from one who does.

Then there are those that think poverty is a deficiency on the part of those who struggle.

Or the antithesis of that thought is that poverty is noble.

What I know to be true is that money and possessions, or the lack thereof, are neither good nor bad. The state of lacking is not noble, nor is state of having evil. It is what you do with the position given that determines your success in life. Your daughter needs to know that as well.

If a child is born into wealth what do they do with that opportunity? If a child is born into poverty how do they achieve from that platform? Then finally, no matter what the economic state of your family is in financial instruction teaches your child how to manage money not let money manage them. There are a couple of lives I find fascinating that I believe exemplify this well.

Florence Nightingale

Named after the city, she was born in—Florence, Italy—Florence Nightingale lived her life in England. Her inspiration crossed oceans and ignited much-needed change within the world of nursing.

Raised in enormous affluence and wealth, she was an extremely educated young woman. Florence's mother was so enamored with the mores of society that she added six bedrooms to their home to accommodate the entertaining she desired when launching her daughters into "society." The two Nightingale daughters were cared for by maids, footmen, and valets;

they traveled between two mansions in England. There was nothing Florence either needed or desired that was not provided for her elaborately and with no consideration of the cost.

However, though Florence traveled with all economic opportunity, she found herself fascinated by social questions of the day and felt called to a different life: "I craved for some regular occupation, for something worth doing, instead of frittering time away on useless trifles."

Such urgings began her exploration of the societal needs of her community, where she visited the homes of the sick. Her discovery of the plight these people found themselves in, led her to seek an answer to their substandard care. She found that the means of change came through the position of nursing.

As her peers attended balls, flirting with young men while sporting new dresses, Florence desired more. The life she sought was to provide care for those who were ill. But, in the early 1800s, the career of nursing was a common one, not respected by affluence. It was women of poverty left with no other option, who took on this job. Her family, thinking it beneath this young lady of position, would not support her desire.

I craved for some regular occupation, for something worth doing, instead of frittering time away on useless trifles. —FLORENCE NIGHTENGALE

Relentless in her purpose, she spent the next fourteen years of consistent persuasion to gain the support of her family to pursue this career. She did not want to defy her parents, yet she could not deny her passion. Finally, with their blessing, she began in a position at the Institution for the Care of Sick Gentlewomen in Distressed Circumstances—simply a hospital for women of poverty. It was there she started her road of social reform. Florence was trained as a nurse while on the job with absolutely no pay from this hospital.

It was in 1844 that she launched her crusade to change the conditions of hospitals after having worked in unbearable circumstances. She found hospitals in squalor with the nursing profession nothing short of low-level maids and determined to singlehandedly reform these institutions.

It was when she headed the nursing unit during the Crimean War that she was able to create real change. This unit was not wanted by the doctors at these British medical facilities, yet she arrived with a party of thirty-eight female nurses at the military hospitals in Turkey. She led her nursing staff as they began the grim and thankless duty of assisting the physicians and caring for the needs of the wounded.

The conditions they found of filth and inefficiency caused the mortality rate of the soldiers to be seven times higher in the hospital than on the battlefield. Miss Nightingale set about to change these by assisting both in setting procedures for receiving incoming supplies as well as the efficiency of care at the hospital. To accomplish this, she used the family relationships and acquaintances she had made while traveling as a young woman. When the war was over, and the nurses sent home, Miss Nightingale personally saw to the financial needs of each nurse, paying them out of her pocket.

As a result of her lifelong struggles with politicians and medical authorities, there was unprecedented reform. Florence used the money subscribed to her name after the Crimean War, not for herself but to establish the Nightingale Home for Nurses. She was the first woman ever to receive the Order of Merit. Nursing as a profession and the sanitary conditions in hospitals, forever changed by the life she chose.

Understandably, Florence Nightingale's life evokes feelings of admiration and respect. But if we look deeply into her specific achievements, we'd find that she probably would not have been able to accomplish such dramatic change if she hadn't been born into wealth. She wouldn't have been able to work without pay while training to be a nurse. Neither would she have been unable to assist her fellow nurses financially at the end of the Crimean War.

There is also a real chance that she wouldn't have been socially prepared to approach political influencers effectively had she not been world traveled. In other words, Florence would have lacked the connections with those same people to seek and gain an audience that enabled her to garner much-needed supplies. She used the printed news to elicit public support—something she would have understood only as a result of her education.

It is from a life of wealth that Florence Nightingale achieved such high results. Is it wrong to have money? No. It is the way in which wealth is viewed and used that can create problems or be the means to solutions.

So, make sure you help your daughter realize that it is not wrong to have money. It is what you do with it. Mothers, this may very well be the place in life you find your family. If so, you must teach your daughter how to manage that financial position. It is not something to create pride or shame. Nor should it be depended upon, since having money holds no real security. It can be here one day and gone the next.

Money truly cannot buy the things that matter in life. But it can be used as a launching pad to achieve accomplishments that the lack of could not. Remember, having money at your daughter's disposal becomes purposeless if she only learns to love the wealth she was born with and not to respect what she can accomplish with it.

Johanna (Anne) Sullivan

It is not only wealth that is considered indicative of what your daughter can become; it is also those born into poverty. This is never to be taught as a determinant of personal success. Poverty does not make life decisions for your child any more than wealth does.

Much has been written about the blind and deaf Helen Keller, but it is her teacher, Anne Sullivan, that I find most interesting. The success she achieved in the life of this disabled child was an inspiration for the untapped potential of many who were considered less capable because of their physical shortcomings. Reading the story of *The Miracle Worker*, one wonders what created the strength and determination of this teacher.

Johanna (Anne) Sullivan was born in Feeding Hills, Massachusetts in 1866 to Irish immigrants. Unfortunately, this family was less than ideal. Her father, an abusive alcoholic, left his children when Anne was a mere ten years of age.

But even before that heartbreaking blow, she suffered a life filled with heartache. Her only brother, Jimmie, was crippled by tuberculosis near birth. At age five Anne was struck with trachoma, leaving her almost blind. Then at age eight, she lost her mother, who died of pneumonia. Their living conditions were those of abject poverty.

Abandoning Anne and her brother to relatives, and then the state "poorhouse" in Tewksbury, Massachusetts, Anne's father permanently left his parental responsibility behind. This institution was for charity cases, including the mentally ill, prostitutes, and those who are incapable of functioning in society. Left with only her brother, Anne was dealt one final family blow. Jimmie died shortly after their arrival at Tewksbury. Anne was truly alone.

The poorhouse had no formal educational program, yet Anne was insistent on learning. Her chance came when Frank Sanborn, chairman of the state board of charities, visited the institution where Anne lived. She followed on his heels relentlessly as he toured the facility, begging for the opportunity to go to the school for the blind.

Mr. Sanborn completed his investigation of the facility at the end of the day, exiting with Anne still pleading to go to school. It was not long afterward that she learned she was to be sent to the Perkins Institute for the Blind. Her persistence had succeeded in Mr. Sanborn acting on her behalf.

Entering the school at age fourteen, unable to read or write and willful from years of neglect, she fought to fit in, often rebelling and struggling with the structure of the school and her peers. As Anne wrote:

I know that gradually I began to accept things as they were, and rebel less and less. The realization came to me that I could not alter anything but myself. I must accept the conventional order of society if I were to succeed at anything. I must bend to the inevitable, and govern my life by experience, not by might-have-beens.

With that disposition, at age twenty she graduated valedictorian of her class. Only six years prior her education had begun without even elementary abilities, yet in the end, Anne was triumphant.

I could not alter anything but myself.
—ANNE SULLIVAN

Not only did she receive an education, several surgeries were performed during her stay at the Perkins Institute for the Blind, Anne's eyesight was regained. Prepared with this sight, her education, and a will to succeed, she took the position as the teacher with the Keller family. And in that job, she accomplished the legendary story in the life of Helen Keller: against the all odds, Anne Sullivan taught a blind and deaf child how to communicate with the world.

It was not only poverty that Anne Sullivan was born into; she had many more struggles to overcome than financial ones. But her story is a motivating one to show that being without is not an excuse to not pursue life success. Poverty does not determine what any daughter can accomplish, and we should not allow it to be portrayed that it does.

If Miss Sullivan had had an easy life, would she have been steeled enough for the battle before her? I think her life is precisely what prepared her for greatness. Financial, physical, or emotional difficulty is not a negative in life; it can be used to shape your daughter's strength of character.

My prayer is that no little girl would ever have to suffer what Anne Sullivan did. That no child would ever experience the heartache, she felt. But if life falls that way for any girl, may she discover what Anne Sullivan learned: "I must bend to the inevitable, and govern my life by experience, not by might-have-beens." Then she can choose a determined path and accomplish more than any less harsh circumstance would ever allow!

Living In-Between

Being rich or poor is not often the issue. Most of us lie somewhere in-between. As a Financial Counselor, you must make sure your girl learns how to manage money and that mismanagement doesn't destroy her. Many young women find, to their shock, that money is controlling their lives; they are not in control of money. Has your daughter begun receiving credit card applications yet? If not, they will soon come. In fact, many colleges in our country allow credit-card companies solicitation access to their students, for a fee. An eighteen-year-old who's clueless about financial management but holds credit cards that will let her spend $3,000 without any means of paying it off is a scary thing indeed.

What's even scarier is that, at eighteen years of age, your daughter can sign an application from the credit card company—or several companies— and suddenly have a billfold of cards at her disposal without you ever knowing. In America today, it's nearly a rite of passage for our daughters, by their early twenties, to get a credit card and charge to the limit.

So, let me make you a little more nervous. According to The Department of Education[11], the end of 2017 showed an outstanding student loan debt in the amount of 1,366.9 Billion dollars. Yes, that is billion! According to a survey conducted by Lendedu[12] the highest percentage of that debt is carried by girls.

So, how do you counsel and plan through this minefield? After all, your daughter is of age, wants to further her education while the credit-card companies will be after her, offering her an easy way to take care of the "I wants." All she has to do, in fact, is fill out a brief application. Higher education is a means to potential future earnings, but at what cost?

O great Financial Counselor, that's why it's so important to teach them about money when they are young!

Because my husband and I worked in our businesses, our vacations were some of the most precious times we had with our daughters. They were often the only times we escaped the demands of work and concentrated solely on our family. Every one of the Brocks looked forward to them.

When it came to vacations, I believed that family memories were imperative, so I was determined to create many. No matter the personal cost, I was committed to the fun.

The year my girls asked me to do a headstand in the pool of the condo we were staying in, I foolishly agreed. I was nearly forty years of age and looked out of my mind with my feet kicking in the air and head underwater. I'm sure I provided an enormous amount of entertainment for the sun-bathers poolside who thought, *What, on earth is that woman doing?*

It took me at least three attempts to get a hand on the bottom of the pool. I could only use one hand because I was holding my nose with the other. The first two attempts I flailed like I was drowning, but the third time I achieved a lopsided, brief, feet-in-the-air handstand to the delight of my girls.

Yes, I'm nuts, but we stored up some great family memories that will be treasured my entire life. Vacations were the fun times…but they also were significant seasons of learning.

Our vacations were never perfect. (Go ahead and admit it: are yours?) There were always downsides to these trips that inevitably held lots of attractions, souvenir shops, and treats. As every parent knows, one of the most stressful days during these family breaks are the "Mommy (or Daddy), can I buy (fill in the blank), can I do (fill in the blank), can I get (fill in the blank)?"

What was the blank? Whatever it was, it cost money. Souvenirs, activities, arcade machines, ice cream—you name it—they wanted to do it all and spend it all. Vacations were like the Niagara Falls of spending.

My husband and I came up with a plan: Why not give our daughters a budget? We thought we were brilliant. Begin the week with a specific dollar amount that we'd give them in cash, and they would have to be responsible for their spending. Well, that year Loren was twelve and Chelsea eight, so of course, as parents, whatever rules you create you have to fulfill. Sticking to the rules became the hard part.

My husband and I came up with a plan: Why not give our daughters a budget? We thought we were brilliant.

That particular vacation where we came up with the budget philoso-phy, was at a beach resort that had this fun arcade on the grounds, and we allowed our daughters to visit it by themselves. They had the cash in hand that we had given them at the beginning of the week with the rules on how it was meant to be used. They could spend the money at their discretion, but they were not to ask us for anymore when this ran out.

Inside the arcade was one of those machines with a crane in it that picked up small stuffed animals. If you put in 50 cents and completed the task, grabbing the animal in the claw to successfully drop it into the depos-itory, it was yours. My youngest was enthralled. This machine awarded stuffed animals and not just a few! In the first three days of a weeklong vaca-tion, she came home with handfuls of little creatures. What we didn't realize was that, by midweek, she'd spent every cent on this challenge.

Wednesday of our vacation week our family went off the resort location to the local souvenir shops. Store to store we walked, perusing the wares that none of us needed but shopped for nonetheless. After all, it was a vacation.

Halfway through our day, Chelsea came up to us with a toy she wanted badly.

Our response? "If you have the money, get it."

The "It's up to you" line was received by a stricken look and immediate tears. Chelsea had no money left; she was broke.

With tears streaming down her face, her father and I took her out of the store to a nearby bench. The sight of my daughter in emotional pain killed me. We found out the child had spent every bit of her money on the arcade and had nothing left for the rest of the week.

As a mom, oh, how I wanted to buy the toy for her, front her some money from her allowance, get her a bank loan, whatever it took. I didn't care. My daughter's heart was breaking.

I mean, I somehow managed, at forty, a headstand in the middle of the pool. Surely, I could find a way to fix this.

One look at my husband and I silently mouthed *I can't do this.* Then I immediately ran for cover, leaving the two of them to discuss her plight. At that moment, I was weak. I knew our daughter needed to learn this lesson, but I was incapable of doing this job. Fortunately, my husband understood my momentary inadequacy and took charge. He explained to her the consequences of her financial decisions and the need to budget her money, as we'd talked about when we'd given it to her. Because she'd already spent her money, she wouldn't be able to buy anything else the rest of the week.

Chelsea cried for a good long while. Finally, I got my resolve back, stepped back into the parenting role, comforted her, and we loaded the car to go back to the resort.

I'm glad we stuck to our original plan. But it was only because, at that moment, my husband was better at this job than I was.

What was incredible is the final result. The next trip our family took Chelsea divided her money equally, using six envelopes for each day of the week. She didn't open them until the appropriate day and even managed to come home with money left over. Chelsea had learned firsthand a lesson in budgeting, and it wasn't one she would forget.

Did this one lesson take care of the spending issue in her life? No, it was only one lesson…but it was effective. And it all happened at a time when my desire was just to have a great time with my family, instead of demanding battles and heartbreak. You see, such lessons happen best when we're "in the trenches" of life.

If your school doesn't teach consumer math, do it yourself. Even if the course is offered, review and reinforce this education with your knowledge. Take the time to instruct your daughters how to buy insurance and why, what a car loan or mortgage is and how much they end up paying in interest, how you use a credit card and how should be used. Make a budget.

And do all of this in a way that works for your daughter. Since girls come with different brain cells and talents, you have to personalize this education. When working on budgets with my daughters, one daughter views life details one way, and the other girl has an entirely different perspective. So, we made the budget accordingly. One understood that things like school supplies, clothing, cosmetics, and cleaning supplies were individual categories. The other daughter had a budget line entitled *Target*. She knew how much she could spend at that store, and that's what she did. Both girls learned that using their cash was a lot better than a credit card. When they ran out of money, they knew they had to quit spending. The few times they ran out of funds early was also a great teacher.

When both our daughters went to college, we helped with spending money in the form of a credit card. We were in a position to do this, and we wanted their education to be their primary focus. I learned the hard way how to manage this commitment. Dinner out with all her new friends on Mom's credit card the first month at college brought the wrath of Mom into my elder daughter's life quickly. She was making new friends, she figured, so why shouldn't she buy their meals as well?

So, I explained *again* that credit cards were for agreed to expenditures, not for random use in college life. The only other charges that were to be made were in the event of an emergency, and dinner out with friends was *not* an emergency.

The new policy we decided on was to transfer money into her checking account twice a month. She had to pay all personal expenses from this account. She also had to subsidize what we gave her with money she earned to meet this cost.

As our daughters were completing college, we transferred more of their overhead to them. At times we helped by increasing our contribution because their earning power was so small. But even though we were still paying for items like health insurance, we did that by adding the money to their income stream from Mom and Dad. Then they had to pay those bills and felt ownership and responsibility by doing so.

Successful Financial Consulting—no matter your financial position—comes down to a few critical requirements.

› Begin early.

› Teach financial responsibility by example first, education next.

› Make sure your girl understands that everything offered is not everything needed. You cannot and must not spend more than you have...at least not without consequences.

› Money is not and should never be the great divider. It will only dictate what you can become if you let debt overtake or wealth dominate.

› And finally, money is a tool, not an answer.

It is your job, Financial Consultant, to teach them to use that tool well. If they do the end caps will be avoided, the credit cards controlled, and your daughters will manage money. Money won't manage them.

-10-

SECURITY OFFICER

| JOB DESCRIPTION |

Security officers provide internal and external protection for their clients, to deter unwanted activity, protecting against intrusion, danger, and harm. Providing private security to evaluate threats effectively, also providing information, and transportation, depending on their clients' needs.

I T IS 3:00 a.m. in Florida and our telephone rings. I stumble out of bed and, utterly incoherent, pick up the telephone. (I already warned you what I'm like first thing in the morning before I've had two cups of coffee; the middle of the night is worse.)

I mumble a hello.

A nearly incomprehensible hysterical voice is at the other end of the line. Waking up quickly, I realize this is my nineteen-year-old daughter, who is attending college in California. And she's sobbing uncontrollably.

Barely making out her words, I find myself terrified, shouting across 3,000 miles of telephone line to get her to calm down. She gathers herself enough to tell me she has just been in a car accident. Now she's walking beside her car barefoot in broken glass, in shock after a front-end collision with another automobile.

Immediately I ask her to sit down. I ask if anyone is with her. Yes, she has a friend in the car.

Is her friend conscious and seated? Yes, she is.

Has anyone called the police? She doesn't know. I'm the first call she made.

Is anyone else there? A weak, shaky voice tells me that a couple drove up, and they are calling the police now.

What about the driver of the other car? She doesn't know.

Are you bleeding anywhere? Only her feet.

How is your car? "The front end is in the dashboard, Mommy," she says.

My heart drops even further. I stay on the phone, trying to remain calm myself to keep her hysteria in check. My husband is sitting up in bed, asking questions that I don't have the answers. We are both wishing this moment was a nightmare from which we would awaken.

The police arrive, then the paramedics. I reluctantly get off the telephone, leaving the work to the professionals who have taken charge of the accident site.

I couldn't have felt more helpless. My daughter was just in a major auto accident, and I was 3,000 miles away.

You have to understand that my husband and I are not faint-of-heart individuals. We have conquered many obstacles in life, often very challenging ones. But we spent the rest of that night roaming the house between telephone calls feeling helpless, knowing we had not one ounce of control over this moment in our daughter's life. There was nothing we could do, and we were in agony.

I have never felt as lost as I did that night. You see, it was my job to protect her. I am her mother.

When a daughter is born, there are two instantaneous emotions: one is love; the other is protection. For me, both were immediate and equally fierce. I was capable of any defense, should someone ever attempt to hurt my girls. I knew at their birth that there was nothing I would not stand against to protect these precious babies. They were mine to keep from harm.

So, in the real world of daughter duties, are we equipped to be the person who would take the bullet? The valiant, without-a-second-thought security officer that leaps in front of the danger heading straight into the heart of your daughter?

The simple answer is yes, we are.

There was nothing I would not stand against to protect these precious babies.

Do we leap into the line of fire? Yes, we do.

Are we always supposed to take that bullet? Stop right there. Now the answer is no.

Do we tackle the offender? Sometimes yes, and sometimes no.

Are we to allow our charges to take a few knocks themselves? Yes, indeed we must.

Are you confused yet? In this job, there are multiple correct answers. You see, the answers change based on the timeline in the life of your daughter, the danger that is present, and each objective.

Here's what I mean. Sometimes the bullets come when your toddler is heading straight toward an open flame, and you throw yourself in front of her, extinguishing the threat. Or you see a car driving down your street as your four-year-old is running after her ball and you perform a body lunge toward her, pulling her from harm. If the danger comes in the form of a boy or a friend, you may have to let your girl take some pain. When she enters the years behind the wheel, you can only be there through the student-driver stage. Then she leaves home for college, and suddenly you can no longer protect her.

If you want to do this job well, you have three goals. First, it is your job to protect. Second, you are to teach them to protect themselves. And finally, if successful, you will have prepared her to protect those she loves when that day comes. The end of a job well done is that your duty will be over. You will be able to retire and relax. After all, when you get arthritic knees, you certainly don't want to try to outrun a grown daughter just to keep her from harm.

Assessing the Dangers

What does this security officer job look like, and what do you have to do? It's easy to envision the human mannequins you've seen in film and television, the ones who provide private security for the stars. You know, the menacing men and women wearing sunglasses, suit, and tie, with an earpiece in their ear and a gun in a holster. They're standing completely still while discretely scanning for any and all potential dangers.

These are intimidating individuals who have learned how to be effective at their job. They shoot well, granted. They are physically fit to run toward danger. They look impressive in their attire. (I don't think that makes a lot of difference, but I couldn't resist the observation.) Their powers of surveillance must be vulture-like. Those great sunglasses are proof of that! All of these, except maybe the clothing, apply.

But the most important ability for the mom version of this security officer is the talent of observation. Keep an eye out for any and all potential harm. Assess its intent and determine the best course of action. Then take the next step to protect or prepare.

The threat that is most spoken of for girls today, the one that brings heartbreak to every mother, is the danger from sexual predators. We see it played out in the media, and it grips all of our hearts with anger and fear.

We have learned that this menace comes from people familiar to us, as well those we don't know. A proficient security officer is not foolish enough to believe that this predator is always an elusive stranger.

When my girls were small, I found this job a difficult balance. While I wanted to educate my daughters to be wary of predators, I also wanted to teach them kindness to all. I didn't want them to replace compassion, vulnerability, and the ability to reach out to others with fear.

If someone approaches your girl saying he lost his puppy, what heartstrings are pulled? Is this a real need for this stranger—or is it a person with ulterior motives? You want compassion to be your daughter's natural instinct while teaching her to recognize the circumstances.

Does the stranger's request make sense—or not? If the request comes from a child, then the dog may truly be lost, and the child may want to help. But if an adult is asking for help, teach your daughter to find another adult. She needs to understand that adults assist other adults; children don't. Place logic in her mind instead of fear.

One thing you can do is to provide her with a safe word. This is a word that you and your daughter have predetermined will indicate safety. It can be any word of your choosing. Make it creative, let your daughter help decide or even make up her special word but one that only the members of your family know. If she finds herself confronted by a stranger and is told that this person knows you or perhaps that you sent this individual to find her, she is to ask the stranger what that word is. If he or she doesn't know her word, then that person doesn't know you. That means she turns tail and runs. Offer this wisdom of caution and the simple steps she needs to take to ensure she will be safe.

Effective Weapons

The most effective weapon in your daughter's arsenal is confidence. This is not just a theory from a mother. A study of criminal behavior in the *Psychology Today* article "Marked for Mayhem[13]" revealed possible deterrents to physical attack. Repeatedly they were told by the criminals interviewed that they were looking for and preying upon those who appear weak, vulnerable, and easily controlled. These became their most likely target. It is proven time, and again that self-confidence works. If your daughter holds her head high, eyes straight ahead, she will look less vulnerable to a predator. If approached, she will act decisively. By not displaying meekness, the chances of an attack drop precipitously. Predators traditionally are not strong humans; they are looking to create strength over the weaker. If your daughter possesses self-confidence, she is armed.

Help her also understand she must always "trust her gut." If she feels something is wrong, if it seems odd or out of place, she should back away. A girl's instinct is reliable. Her best plan is to listen to the first warning bell and act. She will never look back in dismay at the times she thought something was wrong and acted upon her fear even while feeling foolish in her reaction. She'll only regret the times she doesn't listen to her instincts in facing danger.

If your daughter possesses self-confidence, she is armed.

Taking a bullet is simpler for you when your daughter is little. You see the stove, hear the car coming, and know the pool is too deep. When your daughter gets older, taking the bullet can become more difficult. The teen years bring a time of protection in a different form. Your powers of observation have to be even more astute, your line of defense more varied.

Somewhere between twelve and seventeen years of age almost all girls will find a boy or make a friend that potentially brings with him or her a whole bunch of problems.

I hit this milestone with Loren when she was thirteen. She had a girl she met in middle school, as their friendship grew I realized this exciting addition to Loren's life didn't live by any rules. The girl was fun, I liked her, but my insight told me this girl was headed for trouble. Her mother had a pretty loose rein. The thirteen-year-old was left alone in her home until

2 a.m., dated at that ripe young age of 13—and was allowed to date boys much older than she was.

She had very few responsibilities or expectations placed on her in any part of her life. This freedom, along with the fact this middle-schooler was cute and fun, held an irresistible allure for Loren.

Feeling this wasn't the best relationship for my daughter, I tried to impede their friendship. But with each attempt I made to curtail this connection, the stronger it became.

I was in a losing battle…that is until I changed my tactical maneuvers. I began to embrace this girl's presence in our lives. I invited her everywhere on behalf of my daughter: to spend the night, for shopping expeditions, on our day trips, to church, or anyplace else I could make it fit.

I took the tact of "keeping my enemies' closer." Let me be clear: I'm not saying this girl was "the enemy"; she was only a child. But the life she was allowed to live posed a danger to my daughter's well-being.

It didn't take much time before my daughter started making exasperated comments about this newfound friendship. Way too much exposure tarnished the sheen. When her friend was in our world, away from the "glamour" of hers, she didn't seem quite as exciting. Soon their friendship began to fizzle.

I took the tact of
"keeping my enemies' closer."

When I asked Loren if this girl would be joining us, the answer began to be no. The excitement and appeal had faded. The threat had been removed without a throw-down pronouncement by Mom. Had I continued on the road of confrontation, I would have lost. But I protected my daughter in another way.

I cannot guarantee there won't be times when you just have to hit the mat to win the battle. There will be. But if you can find another route toward success, it's less painful for all.

Nothing, In Life, Is Fail-Proof

Protecting your daughter isn't fail-proof. We teach our children how to treat burns if they happen, how to call the police and exchange information if in an auto accident. We try to instill the value of the 9-1-1 telephone call, which of course my nineteen-year-old didn't use. In her panic, she did the only thing she could remember to do: she called home. Know this; even if they don't always default to what we teach, we do well when we provide real-world instruction for the simple problems.

It is protection from your daughter's opportunity to be harmed that require much more. Sometimes tactical maneuvers on your part work; sometimes they don't. The best way to assist your daughter in protecting herself is to limit her exposure. Help her avoid scenarios that introduce her to compromise.

When I was seventeen, my weekend curfew was 12:00 p.m. I had friends who were allowed to stay out past that hour, so I fought my parents valiantly and nonstop to change that rule. They would not bend. One night, when arguing again with my father, he posed a question to me: "What can you do or where can you go after 12:00 that doesn't lead to trouble?"

I stumbled. Most movies were over; concerts had let out; ball games and school dances had ended. I could say, "Just hang out with my friends," but I knew that wouldn't fly. I couldn't give him a good answer because there wasn't one.

My curfew remained, and that day I quit arguing. My father was smart; he kept me from making bad decisions by limiting the opportunity.

The questions my teenage daughters always had to answer were: Where are you going, with whom, and what time will it be over? They had to provide the detail before they left home, and if plans changed, they had telephones and were instructed to inform us immediately. Information was king at the Brock Family Home.

I also told them I knew they could tell me in great detail what their plans were and the moment they left the house they could be anywhere with anyone doing anything. Without a satellite-tracking device, a tracking device I placed on their phone or an accidental meeting, I wouldn't know the difference.

So, I made it clear to them that I knew that. Part One of our policy was that our teenagers were implicitly given our trust—that we believed they would tell us the truth. Now, we weren't delusional, we knew that being truthful in all circumstances was incredibly unrealistic. After all, they were teens. But we felt that it was essential to establish our level of expectation, the information provided should meet the standard that we had set.

But there was a Part Two to that policy: should we ever find out they lied to us, that trust would be lost...and it would be a long, agonizing journey ever to regain it.

This choice was theirs.

So, make rules (this falls back on the Coach job). Set reasonable, easily understood, and concrete guidelines for curfews, age-appropriate entertainment, what friends can be in their car, seatbelt use, and other parental oversight when appropriate. Be willing to set the rules.

But as you set them, also be willing to listen. You want your daughter to know you are reasonable and rational. If her curfew is 12 p.m., and she has worked at the fast-food restaurant until her 9 p.m. shift ends, you need to allow her to make a presentation. She and her friends are getting a burger, then going to the 10:20 movie premiere that they have all been waiting to see. With drive time, which means not speeding and dropping off her best friend, she can't make it home until 12:55.

Should you stick to the rules because they are the rules? Say, "No, absolutely not. 12:55 is past your curfew!"? Your daughter has a job for heaven's sake! She is being responsible and presenting her case. So, give it to her! Your focus should be on building mutual respect and training your daughter to become an adult, not merely setting rules that must be rigidly adhered to, no matter what.

The day will arrive when she will be on her own; she must be prepared to protect herself. Helping her build good decision-making skills will help her do this. Part of bending your rules when appropriate creates the ability in your daughter to make these sound decisions.

Preparation Is Your Best Defense

If you have ever watched dog trainers, they keep the dog on a short leash until they learn. Then slowly, over time, the dogs are given room to maneuver.

The same is true for our daughters: you want to give them the ability to make their own decisions. The rules established at thirteen aren't the same as at age fifteen, which aren't the same as at age eighteen. I've seen many kids in the most stable homes hit college and party until the sun comes up. Why? because they were overprotected and they were underexposed. They weren't allowed to experience life, pain, and just grow up. They arrived unprepared for the sudden freedom thrust upon them.

Instead of learning decision making while they were in the safety of their parents' home, they only knew instruction; being told what to do, how to do it and when it should be done. Now suddenly they were free to do whatever they wanted, whenever they wanted, anyway they chose. When their decision-making muscles aren't exercised when they are under their parent's roof, they are under-developed, not trained to make good decisions within their newly discovered freedom.

There is not a mother who wants our daughters to suffer heartache, disappointment, and punishment, but here's the catch: they *must*. We cannot forever insulate our girls from the sadness and evil of our world. They have to experience childhood peer rejection, pain, and distress to prepare them for adult peer rejection, pain, and distress.

A Security Officer protects, but if she is really good, she also teaches self-defense.

Allowing them in the right season to gain insight on other people, as well as knowledge of society, is necessary preparation for independence. We cannot come between them and life because most of their life lessons are through experience. Those lessons cannot be explained or instructed; your girl has to live them. As much as we would like, we cannot raise our daughters in a bubble, then thrust into the real world and expected to handle it. We have to train them much as you do an athlete. Each time they gain an ability, they should learn a new skill. The old "no pain no gain" applies to emotional strength as much as physical strength.

I have a limited view of running. It would only become necessary in my life should I be chased. Fear of harm is the only thing that would drive me to run. I can't think of another good reason to get my legs going that fast. But I love watching runners at the Olympic Games. They are so lean, muscular, disciplined, and determined. When they run, it looks so effortless. They *fly*.

The ultimate fun is the 4 x 100 relay. This race is a combination of four runners, each set appropriately in position to make the most of their running ability to then hand off the baton to the subsequent runner for their leg. The race ends with everyone rooting for the final competitor sprinting for the finish line. But to win, it takes all team participants excelling at their leg of the race and completing the hand-off to the next runner flawlessly. They have to train and train well to be a part of this team.

Initially, it requires them to become one of the best runners individually. Strength and speed achieved as they go through levels of training. Beginning naturally at a slower pace, they practice running and achieve endurance. Then they undergo weight training to gain strength to ensure that the body's muscles are powerful enough to maintain the demands placed upon them. After becoming a proficient runner competing individually, they vie for the privilege of being a member of the relay.

The runners look to their coach to determine what place in the race they are most suited. Training again but no longer alone, they work to perfect the handoff of the baton. This process takes time, commitment, and determination by the runner and coaching by a competent instructor. Finally, after years of preparation, they become a cohesive team that can function smoothly as one entity.

In the same way, you as mom go from the pure taking of the bullet to teaching self-defense. Then you move from teaching defense to committed character building. You, Mom, are one leg of the race, and your goal is to train your daughter to be strong enough to run her leg of the race well.

It is not only overprotection or underexposure, that may leave a girl vulnerable to wrong choices, it is also her free will. You will provide her instruction, but you cannot control all of her choices. As your daughter walks through her teen years, stepping into adulthood, there is this reality; choices will be hers to make, some of them will be great, others will not. Lifestyles adopted, and compromises embraced may be ones that you understand are harmful. Our daughters will make their share of mistakes; we are foolish if we think they won't. I certainly made my own in life, and you can't tell me in all honesty that you missed out on that one yourself.

If those days come, you may experience deep sadness, loss, disappointment and even guilt. But I want to give every one of you mothers a break, there is only one perfect parent, God, and even his kids rebelled. It happens to the best of us.

There was a time of heartbreak in my life that I needed to gain understanding; because I had none. It was the year my father struggled with severe depression, which led to him taking his life. I felt unbelievable loss and confusion. It was then that I was offered this phrase, "Don't mistake the man for the moment." It was a simple statement that encouraged me never to let that one moment in time define the entirety of his life. He was and still is a father worthy of love, respect, and admiration. This truth carried me through many difficult days.

The same is true for our girls. You may be in a season of difficulty. You are watching as your daughter makes choices that you know will come with a cost they may yet be unaware. Do not, I repeat, do not mistake this season for the nature, character or potential of your girl. Do not focus on the challenge of today to the exclusion of the beauty that lies within her. Be the one who still knows the incredible girl she is, with a heart of hope for tomorrow. What is challenging today may very well be what will make her into the strong woman that she will become.

The day will come when your daughter enters the world of adulthood; it is then that you, Security Officer. Will retire the duties of protecting. But you never leave the job of standing by your charge, encouraging her and believing in her, even when she places herself in perilous and vulnerable situations.

---

*Train your daughter to be strong enough
to run her leg of the race well.*

When they are defying our principals or simply clamoring to get out on their own, we often take it personally. A Security Officer? He or she just moves on to a new job. Hard to do that as a mother, isn't it? But there's something to be learned about this role. While we really will miss our daughters when they leave, we *want* them to leave. And no, I don't mean getting them out of the house so they're no longer underfoot (though some days, in the heat of the moment, that might be a bonus). Instead, we want them to be complete, competent humans who can make it on their own. Sometimes it takes leaving home to figure out how to become those girls we know they can be.

One of the final stages of protection and preparation comes in the nuances of society—the areas of life that can be difficult to define and where gray areas often seem appropriate.

We, Brocks, were parents who demanded and expected personal responsibility from ourselves as well as our children. So, when faced with our younger daughter's interest in taking an Ethics Class at the local college, we had apprehensions.

Chelsea was a senior in high school, completing her education at an "institution of higher learning"—the college in our community. We were savvy enough to know that the ethics taught at the public institution would in no way resemble our position or values, but she wanted to take the class so, with some trepidation, we signed on.

The course description included absolute and relative systems, ethical issues in contemporary society, defining ethical judgments and refining them. We could have run from this influence, but we determined it would challenge and prepare her for many life confrontations in the area of ethical or moral stances.

Before she began, we discussed the possibilities of the course-work, and what she would learn. She listened (I'm sure mentally rolling her eyes, thinking we were so overreacting). Then began the class. Indeed, she heard that there are no moral absolutes. What is considered correct in one culture is not in another, was the philosophy, so how any one set of rules can be right was not conclusive. There were the issues of life value, religious influence on moral culture and its relevance, and simple questions such as, "Is there a time when a lie is appropriate?"

We had many discussions at our home regarding these subjects. When is it right to take another person's life? I had to admit that if anyone were trying to remove my child from my home to inflict harm that would be the time I'd be tempted to take a life.

Is it ever okay to lie? Those who saved lives during the Holocaust lied, yet their cause was nobler than truth. They saved others from torture and death by their deceit.

In hindsight, I'm delighted Chelsea took this class. It challenged her. She worked through many issues. Not all were resolved, but they were weighed. It would have been wrong to run from something that we thought dangerous to our daughter's moral character. You see, Chelsea has always been a child who makes discoveries, seeks information, and wants to learn. She is curious about other people's opinions—how they formed them and why. This subject was no different. It was not a denouncement of all she had learned from us, but a step toward creating and confirming her thoughts as she grew toward adulthood.

If our daughter didn't face the issues in that class, at a time when she could discuss her thoughts and questions with us, in the safe setting of our home, we knew that she would address them later, in another time, in another way. And she might not have the support of others who shared our family's values. So, we were there as parents in an open forum, discussing all she was learning. We did resolve many of the questions she developed during this course study because we allowed that opportunity in her life while were by her side.

Through the exercises and discussions, we didn't always agree. Chelsea had her own opinions. And what's even crazier is that she was right in some of those disagreements. Remember: you want a daughter, not a clone. She must figure out the issues for herself, but if you do your job, her judgments will be more often right than wrong.

Your Job Is to Protect—At All Costs

Overprotection is a problem, we are all aware of the "helicopter parent" phenomenon, but complete destruction comes from others who have discarded the responsibility to protect. News stories tell of many mothers who allow physical abuse in their home. They may choose a husband, boyfriend, or relative over their daughters, feeling helpless to change a dangerous situation. Looking the other way, they abandon their priority: to protect their daughters. It is in no one's best interest to remain in a place where violence, physical or verbal, is dispensed. This is destructive not only to the mother but the entire family and must end.

I watch as the entertainment industries increasingly seek younger performers. I am astounded by the mothers who encourage their daughters in the fields of performance. They often allow these young girls to set aside their self-esteem for "success." Placing a vulnerable child in the way of a manipulative entertainment industry without guarding their best interest is unforgivable.

Child stars often damaged by the world they are exposed to the day their parents quit being parents. I'm not saying that you should deny your child the opportunity that may be right for who they are to become. But it is imperative to remain the *parent* in that world.

Children are still-developing humans who require protection, rules, discipline, education, and fun to grow up to be a functioning adult. Industry standards should never supersede parental standards in a child's life, no matter how "successful" they are. The first rule of order is a simple one, the parent rules—no one else.

Children are sometimes left alone to care for themselves. The damage done when a child is unattended while a mother goes elsewhere, seeking pleasure and fulfillment, is unconscionable. I want to be clear that this is not a commentary on the *working* mother (after all, I was one myself all the years my daughters were growing up) but on the *selfish* mother, who is acting solely her own best interests and not considering what is best for her child.

The first rule of order is a simple one,
the parent rules—no one else.

Security Officers with their various clients have to sign a contract. One that often includes the character of the officer, one who is "worthy of trust and confidence." So why shouldn't mothers have to sign a contract when birthing or adopting a child? We moms must intentionally choose to conduct ourselves with the same moral integrity as required of others who are fulfilling this role.

So, Officer, how do we provide security, protect and prepare?

Do we leap into the line of fire? Yes, we do.

Are we always supposed to take that bullet? No.

Do we always tackle the offender? Yes and no.

Are we to allow our charge to take a few knocks themselves? Yes, we are.

You must protect, teach, and prepare your daughter, then send her off to fulfill her destiny with the ability to manage life well without you by her side. And here's the long-term perk for you: if you do that, you are out of a job—at least one of them, Security Officer.

-11-

COMMUNICATIONS SPECIALIST

| JOB DESCRIPTION |

Mastery in the art of communication: responsible for the application of techniques used to apply words effectively. Able to provide instruction in the tools needed to impart information or ideas successfully. Must possess the ability to transmit information to ensure open, interactive, and effective communication skills.

WE, THE FEMALE gender, have been given an exceptional talent. We are incredible in our ability to communicate, to impart information, to secure effect. We use words in abundance. If we are honest, it is not a sentence used to complete our thoughts, but paragraphs.

We can convince others of our point of view or inspire someone to action, with the sheer quantity of information that comes out of our mouths. Sometimes I believe it may not be the fantastic content but the pure volume itself. Surrender may come out of nothing less than exhaustion on the part of those to whom we are speaking.

You see, words are our strength. They are also our weakness. If not used correctly, this gift can be the most damaging human weapon known to humankind. Since our verbal ability is instinctive, we often use words without thought, leaving a path of destruction we may not even see. We might pride ourselves on the ability to say what is on our mind, without holding back. We might believe that it is our responsibility to set things straight...no matter what. When words are efficiently wielded as a sword over someone else, they can leave in their wake devastation, humiliation, hurt, and heartbreak.

Words are our strength.
They are also our weakness.

Words can be a lethal weapon, and all women know their strength. That's why it's critical we become Communications Specialists early, training ourselves in the art of speaking. Otherwise, our own words can cause death. I'm not talking about the end of our physical existence, but the death of relationships, opportunity, friendship, and family strength. All in life that is good and valuable can be degraded by thoughtless remarks or by purposeful comments that have veiled but malicious intent.

The Wisdom of Solomon

King Solomon, whom I continue to be fascinated by, appeared to have absolutely no understanding of women. Marrying as many women as he did and keeping them all near his home in a harem solidifies the fact that the wisest man who ever lived was at least at some point in life clueless.

Can you imagine the things said among Solomon's wives at their residence?

"Oh, that hairstyle looks wonderful. It's a very appropriate style for a woman of *your* age."

Or maybe something like this: "That was such a thoughtless remark from her. Oh, you didn't hear it? Well, just know *I* would never have said that about you."

Then imagine the harem concern for another in their ranks: "We're so dismayed about how she raises that son. The way she pampers him"—heads shake—"and to think he is supposed to be the king's heir. It's so sad that he certainly won't be fit for the throne."

And the one wife to another wife (if our brain can even go there) statement: "I overheard the eunuch, and he said I'm the king's favorite. I don't know why he likes me so much when you're so special too."

A conclave of women vying for importance in the royal household filled with conniving, dangerous, and ugly words cloaked in prettiness. The sole husband of all those wives proved that somewhere in life he came to understand these creatures he brought into his kingdom when he expounded nuggets of incredible wisdom. His observations regarding women and the effect of their words are profound.

Take these for example:

A quarrelsome wife is like a dripping faucet.

Or as we might say: Continuous nagging is seriously irritating, and anyone living with that would pay a plumber any amount of money to make it stop.

Better to live on the corner of the roof than share a house with a quarrelsome woman.

Or as we might say: Your husband, sitting in his recliner in front of the big screen TV, is contemplating that living on the roof in the rain would be better than hearing you complain about one more thing.

Better to live in the desert than with a contentious and angry wife.

Or as we might say: A dry, sandy, hot, miserable desert lined with cacti looks like a great place to be when arguing and dissatisfaction is the only thing that ever comes out of your woman's mouth.

Solomon did figure out how challenging the women he brought home could become, and as many men, often too late in the relationship.

The Misuse of Words

We are delighted when our baby girls add to their vocabulary in their distinct way. They form words that only we can decipher. The sentences with one word, then two or three words, then move to whole sentences, and finally, never-ending paragraphs. It's when the words get strung together that things can get ugly. The sweet "mommy, doggie, teddy bear" words turn into "no, I don't want to; get me down; that's mine"—all said, of course, at the top of their lungs.

Effective Communications Specialists realize that defiant, resistant phrases have to be addressed at that very early age. It's not only the words our daughters learn but what lies behind them.

When you are unloading the car, and she is impatient to get out of the car seat, she must ask, not scream and demand. A child who barks commands to her mother and gets by with it is being trained to be controlling. The art of effective communication is learning *how* to say things to accomplish the results you want.

If we respond to demands acting upon our daughters' directive, they will learn this is the way to get whatever they want. Then the only forms of request your child knows are screaming, demanding, and insisting, and I can guarantee you she will use those to the very best of her ability.

So, teach your child not only *how* to ask—nicely—for what she wants but also make it clear there is a time she needs to stop asking, even if the answer you give isn't what she wants to hear. It may look like, to others, that you are merely trying to curb the attitude of a little one, but it is much more than that. An adult woman will communicate using whichever communication skills she's been taught and developed throughout her growing-up years. It's one thing for a two-year-old to demand action loudly and belligerently; it's a whole other thing for a forty-two-year-old to do it. It just ain't pretty.

No!

This simple two-letter English word can be the most rebellious statement made by your precious two-year-old. Granted, that word has been a constant one she's heard for the last eighteen months from you, the mother. The first time she reaches for something harmful, you say no. When she pulls your hair, you say no. When she throws food across the kitchen, you say no.

But your daughter's no is done with a different kind of attitude. When you ask her to pick up her toys, and she looks straight into your eyes as she declares, "No!" you feel the full impact of her defiance. What does her "No!" really mean? It means, "Ain't no way, Mama, and I dare you to make me do it."

What does verbal defiance, if not curbed in childhood, accomplish for an adult woman? It gets her nowhere. Others avoid her, appease her, and skirt around her issues rather than engaging. So, now's the time to nip "No" in the bud, no matter what age your daughter is.

Mine!

Mine is a simple, four-letter, possessive pronoun. But it speaks volumes. One of my daughters had a cloth doll that went everywhere with her. During the day it was dragged around the house; it was always in her bed at night. My daughter and that doll were inseparable. She would lay in bed twirling her hair, saying, "Lolly doll is my friend. She is my baby" and other sweet, endearing phrases.

It was in daycare that I first saw the other version of "mine" from this little girl. As I walked into the class to pick her up, a little boy reached for her doll.

And from my sweet angel's lips came an ear-piercing shriek: "MIIIINN-NNE!!!" (Note triple exclamation marks.) Quickly picking up the toy truck he had left behind, she promptly hit him over the head to make sure he understood the meaning of that word.

He did. Then, he cried as I strode across the playroom, scooped my daughter up, and scolded her action. I tried to make my daughter understand that this behavior was completely unacceptable and made it clear that she needed to tell him she was sorry and ask for forgiveness from the little boy.

After that process, the little boy settled down and appeared relatively unscathed, so my daughter and I went home to continue this discussion, as well as pursue the appropriate discipline for her action. The intention behind this word then was anything but endearment. It was selfish vehemence on my girl's part.

The "mine" in an adult female is present in both hearts and vocabularies. But it's most often couched in sentences so innocuous that they are often unidentifiable. It's no longer the obvious screeching of a demanding little girl, but a statement made about something we want that is only our desire or best interest.

I believe in my husband's, and my wedding vows we should have added: "I, Darlene, will never add floral prints, lace curtains, or girlie colors in our home." Now I'm not a floral-print, lacey kind of female, but if I were, my husband would have been miserable in his own home. I've seen that kind of décor in homes where a hunting, fishing, spitting kind of guy resides. I believe these screams "mine" in the grown-up world because indeed the home front should be the epitome of marital compromise and unselfish actions. It doesn't matter how many times you say or convince yourself the home is beautiful if it is beautiful only to you.

"I want what I want and nothing less" can be delivered with a smile, by stubbornness, through sex, through stony silence, or other ways a female can use to make clear what she wants and to get her way.

So, when you find yourself falling into such behavior, take a step back. Is the possessive, selfish intention of your presentation clear? Do you want this just because your intent is "mine"—or because it's the right thing to do for your family?

The "no" and "mine" are all simple word lessons to be taught when your child is young and just beginning the verbal barrages. As in every other life instruction you give to your daughter, managing the words she uses must come early, consistently reinforcing how you want her to speak.

Belittling

I believe that all women every day of their lives have to battle the misuse of words. Words are something we are so good at that we will fall prey to abuse. We must recognize that the most significant instruction for our daughters will be the very words we speak.

Back to the words of Solomon: *A wise woman builds her house, but with her own hands a foolish one tears hers down.*

Often our homes are destroyed by us. Never do we bring in the bull-dozer, raise the sledgehammer, or wield the ax; it is our words that we use to accomplish the demolition. It is those words our daughters must be instructed to guard against.

There are many things said by mothers that simply make me sad. One of the most heartrending and distressful is when you hear a mother belittle her child. The casual or angry phrases we are capable of speaking destroy our daughters' self-confidence and decry the relationship of love between a child and their mother.

I'm not saying we should tell them constantly they are beautiful, brilliant, and perfect 24/7. They aren't. But we should not demean their look, their actions, or their words. We should build them up. We can help our daughters rise above difficult circumstances just by our support and love. What they think of themselves will significantly be based on what we have said to them.

If we say they are smart, they will believe they are.

If we say they are stupid, they will believe that as well.

If we tell them they can accomplish a difficult task, they will believe they can.

If we tell them a challenge is too much for them, they will believe that, too.

What they think of themselves will greatly
be based on what we have said to them.

Have you heard women speak to or about their men with superiority and disdain? Words that disparage the character and nature of a man only serve to destroy the promising relationship that began on their day of commitment. As with your daughters, not everything your man does is worthy of accolades (everything you do isn't either).

But as much as it is true that a man needs his wife to believe in him, it is equally true that if a wife's words indicate contempt, a husband's self-confidence, and self-esteem can be is undermined. When feeling of little worth, he is left with two choices. The first is to live his life seeking, at all costs, to make peace in his home—subsequently losing himself in the process. The second is to look elsewhere for someone who encourages his self-worth.

Words are powerful—far more powerful than you could ever imagine. And the consequences of your words are far-reaching in every area of life, but especially in the arena of family.

Let me be blunt. Since we, as women, are often motivated by self-preservation, why would we *choose* to drive a husband away by our words? After all, you can count on the fact that there is a woman in your man's life who is willing and desiring to fulfill whatever he is seeking. A sure way to destroy a marriage is to change from treating the man you married as one of your life's treasure to debris that is without value and readily discarded.

And always remember: how you speak to your daughter's father will most likely be how your daughter speaks to her man too. You by your words will serve to prepare her for success or failure in her relationships. If you are not currently married, don't skim over this section. Your daughter does have a father who is a vital part of her life. Your words to him should be words you don't ever regret. This also applies to your relationships with all men. Building good relationships is based on these same principles, and the effect will be the same.

How you speak to your daughter's father
will most likely be how your daughter
speaks to her husband.

The gossip line

Finally, there is the friend that betrays another, words that are unkind, or gossip shared with someone else for reasons that can never be justified. Women deliver these words. They are cloaked with concern when the motivation is not that whatsoever. The classic phrase "I'm so concerned about Jessica" is frequently followed with information about Jessica that should never be shared...successfully cloaking gossip in false compassion. I hate the next phrase that often follows with people of faith: "I wanted you to know so you could pray for her." Now REALLY, this should drive any kindhearted woman into insanity. We can pray without ever knowing all the details!

All women have been the victim of the "concerned words" that with a different intent behind them. These are some of the most hurtful of all because others who shouldn't know anything about your situation are suddenly informed of the blow-by-blow details, all under the guise of "helping you." Ladies, let's keep private information private.

And don't fool yourself: every woman is capable of forming them. That means even you, even me, even your daughter. Used to manipulate a situation or debase another, these are the most effective, while seeming innocuous. They usually begin with Part A, the pleasant part, and end with Part B, the dangerous part of the conversation.

"That dress makes you look so much thinner than normal." Which is it exactly? Do I look thin or normally look fat?

"I love your new hair color. It's so much better than the old one." So, did you hate my hair before?

"Your kids are so much better behaved at school." Does that mean they are a mess while you are in your living room or at the mall? Is the teacher better than you with your child? So, what exactly are you saying here?

These examples are a few of the fairly mild sentences that can confuse and unnerve the one being spoken to. Often these are said without thinking or without the perceived intent, but we should guard against these as well. We females of all ages are frequently an insecure bunch, and one of these thoughtless remarks can send an emotionally stable lady into a tailspin. Your daughters will find these phrases come out of their mouths, as you have yourself. Just make sure you teach them that Part A is always good enough on its own.

A thoughtless remark can send
an emotionally stable lady into a tailspin.

The ultimate application of Communications Specialists is this: Do not let your daughter *ever* speak to you using words that you would never say to her. The words used, as well as the attitudes behind those words, must fit this criterion. Adopting this home policy will not only help your daughter think through her words but will make you conscious of yours.

I'm not saying there won't be stormy days from both sides of the family. My daughters have stomped up the stairs declaring they are furious at me.

My response? "Well, no problem whatsoever, because I'm angry at you too." Anger, frustration, and disagreement are not wrong; it's what is said at those moments that can damage.

Your words will bring life or death in the relationship between a mother and daughter.

The Power of Words

The reason our words have such impact is that we were made to communicate. We have the incredible ability to change the world, the ability to persuade for good. There have been countless women in history who have understood this power and mastered words to achieve a needed end. Let me give you a few examples of how true that can be.

Harriet Beecher Stowe

Harriet Beecher Stowe, the author of *Uncle Tom's Cabin,* written in 1852, used her ability to communicate to solidify the residents of the North against slavery. She recognized an injustice, then followed the dictum of her father, who said, "If you see a wrong, right it."

"If you see a wrong, right it."
—HARRIET BEECHER STOWE'S FATHER

It was one Sunday afternoon that Harriett passionately put on paper the story inspired by a vision she received in the church that very morning. This work when completed portrayed slaves as human beings that were no less significant and purposed than their white counterparts. Selling 300,000 copies in its first year, the publication quickly achieved its goal. Ms. Stowe's work began the course of developing understanding; each race was truly equal helping set the platform that would bring change. Her words on paper activated the north to right this wrong.

Laura Ingalls Wilder

Laura Ingalls Wilder, writer of the *Little House on The Prairie* series along with her daughter/editor, released the first book in 1932. These books portrayed the pioneer culture and the hardships that forged opportunity in our land. Creatively and entertainingly, we found ourselves walking through a time lost to our nation. That mental journey mirrored strength of character in a territory settled through determination. Today the simplicity of the era portrayed in these books still inspires young generations to dream of a life different from what they know and believe they too can forge new paths.

Flannery O'Connor

Author Flannery O'Connor has used the American novel to explore human alienation and the relationship with an individual God. Depicting the tragic nature of humanity, she profoundly succeeds in challenging the most secure of thinkers. Her work, while sometimes sad and forlorn, creates thought-provoking questions that cry out for answers.

Words of life

Words can bring change, provide comfort, understanding, security, strength, and resolve. These and many other American authors, speakers, and women from all walks of life have changed the country we live in with only their words. Masterfully creating awareness and inspiring reflection, these communicators convince others to believe in themselves. They stir the hearts of many who then become catalysts for change in the world around them. Words of life are what we want to communicate to our daughters. We must also teach them how to use such words of life—as well as when to speak and when to say nothing.

I love the statement by British writer Dorothy Nevill that brings the value of speaking well to life: "The real art of conversation is not only to say the right thing at the right moment but to leave unsaid the wrong thing at the tempting moment."

Phrases and sentences offered to encourage others to seek purpose, to feel valued, and to be loved. These will be instructive and corrective when stated in a well-thought-out, humble manner. And not only the ability to speak but the ability to listen will make our words much more valuable. If you have taught this to your daughter, she will be made better by her own words and others will benefit from them as well.

It was the living room of my great grandmother's home on Saturday nights where I waxed most eloquent at five years of age. I'd be standing at the small podium she owned directly in front of the red horsehair sofa. With great flourish and drama, I would place the family Bible upon the lectern, opening it to some page (I didn't yet know how to read). There I began my Saturday night sermons.

The stories would grow, taking many turns and forms. I would raise my voice like the preacher I heard in Sunday morning church and expound. My finger would point in the air; my arms would flail. I would walk beside the "pulpit" with confidence to make my point, then return to the text, staring intently at the page I could not read.

My diminutive grandmother would sit in her housedress with hands in her lap, eyes glued to my every move. She listened attentively. As my stories got bigger and grander, she would nod and agree. When I became quiet and thoughtful in my delivery, she seemed to hang on every word I said. My prose was windy, often confused in direction, but always filled with adjectives. I believed I was the grand orator and my audience was enthralled.

And when I ended, I walked away with far more than just believing I'd made an excellent presentation that day.

My grandmother treated what I had to say as important, worthy of her time and attention. She made me feel that every word I said mattered. I believed, in those moments, that I had something to share that was worthy of attention…that *I* was worthy of notice. Her attentiveness gave me the confidence that my words could change the world.

She made me feel that
every word I said mattered.

The truth is, words can. Communications Specialist, be that lady who sits on the sofa listening. Or let your daughter chatter in the kitchen during meal preparation, expounding on whatever she values that day. If your daughter believes her words matter and learns how to use them for good, they will have an immense impact. Then she, indeed, can change the world. Just watch her!

12

IN-HOME DEMONSTRATOR

| JOB DESCRIPTION |

Professionally arrange, display, and present products in household venues to illustrate the quality of the product line and how to use it. Effectively communicate the need for, and value of the product presented.

"**M**OM ON STRIKE!" Through time, mothers have had the urge to strike: to walk out on the job and renegotiate for better terms. Placing a placard on the front lawn of a normal home in Middle America sounds so very appealing sometimes, doesn't it? This large sign could be set to remain front and center until changes are made in your family's life.

Well, that's precisely what the mother of a dear friend of mine did. She placed that sign in her front yard. It remained for more than one month while she went on strike.

Late one night, as we young mothers were weary and expounded on the happenings of our day, my friend told me this tale about her mother. She explained that she didn't understand when she was young, why her mother took a very unusual stand. But now that she had children of her own, what her mom had done all those years ago finally made sense.

This was the act of a mother desperate for change. A mother who had the tremendous load of caring for a home, a husband, and two teenage children. Not only was there a sign in the front yard, but there was also one in the laundry room, and one placed prominently on the kitchen cabinets. Occasionally, just to ensure the full effect and create the personal embarrassment of this teenage daughter, the slogan was carried by her mother while walking back and forth on the sidewalk in front of their home. To the total horror of this teenage girl, her mother made a point of making that march just as the school bus dropped her at the corner of their block.

As in the case of all mothers of teens, this mother was frustrated. She had picked up dirty clothes from the floor once too often. She had spanned the distance between the sink and dishwasher to relocate the dirty dishes created by her children, placing them where they should have been. That distance might as well be the Grand Canyon of teenage years. For some incomprehensible reason, the forty-two-inch trek is just too much for any teen to traverse when it comes to putting away the evidence of their late-night snacks. The open food on the counter, books left scattered around the house, trash cans full to overflowing, dirty clothes inside out when dirty or on the floor when clean—simply stated, the ingratitude of her children was more than this mother had signed on for.

So, she went on strike. For one very long month, she didn't clean, cook the meals, change sheets, do the laundry, or shop for groceries. There was absolutely nothing she had done previously caring for her family that she did while on strike.

The ingratitude of her children was more than this mother had signed on for.

My friend recounted that, after only two weeks, their home was disgusting. Laundry was piled high, there were no clean dishes available, and trash was overflowing. The refrigerator was bare; schoolbooks lost in the debris. With a commitment from the father to support his wife and not touch a thing, the only clean room in the house was the parents' bedroom, and they retreated there often. These teenagers were being forced to determine if they were going to give in.

Of course, they weren't going to surrender. After all, weren't all these things part of the mom's job?

It took one more extraordinarily long and dirty week of the family stand-off before any action was taken. The two teen children were confident their mom would give in and they would not.

I give this mom a lot of credit. Even though she hated messes, she was equally determined. She would not surrender.

By Friday evening, on the third week of this strike, my friend sneaked into the bedroom of her younger brother, and they discussed the fact that they could no longer live this way. They made a plan to relent the following day and clean the house. Saying nothing to anyone else in the family, they decided they would at least lay down their arms for one day.

It took that entire Saturday, well into the evening, to get the place back into any reasonable shape. These two teenagers did kinds of work that they had previously been unexposed. Washing every dish in the house, tackling the never-ending laundry, vacuuming, dusting, and mopping were all done that day by these two.

This very wise mother said not a word when she saw them begin the job. She quietly left the house and had a day away. I know if I had been that mother, I would have walked out that door, driven away from the seeing eyes in my home, then yelled "Bravo, well-done mom!" in absolute unbridled elation. I'd have pulled the car over and then, to the consternation of my neighbors (who already would have thought I'd gone over the edge of insanity for putting up the sign on my front lawn in the first place), hopped out of the car and danced on the curb. In my eyes, what was taking place back on that home front would be nothing short of a miracle.

But that mom didn't end her strike that day. She was smart enough to realize that one cleaning day did not a change make. It was their commitment to *sharing* household duties that she wanted to achieve. She hadn't come this far for her teenagers to think that was the end of the battle. To their surprise, they were required to continue on the cleaning track, which they did. It wasn't until ten days later that she took all of her placards down. After a family meeting, with a settlement of workload shared by all members in writing, she went back to work. Her job caring for the family was still the one that accomplished the most, but for the first time, her children realized what that job took.

Did that one experience mean the end of dirty dishes and clothes on the floor? No. But what it created was an understanding in this family of the duties their mother performed. It also put more responsibility in the hands of each family member.

While we inevitably hold the primary caretaking role on the home front (life experience tells me this is true whether we like it or not!), we are *mothers*. We are not *slaves*. This holds true whether we are stay-at-home moms, or our jobs take us outside of the home. It's just a natural fact; women see the things that need to be done. Our line of vision is broad in the caretaking front; we notice even when no one else does. This fact shouldn't be feared or run from. It's a good thing. Someone in the family has to see what needs to be done and then find a way to manage this responsibility with the help of all. But this knack of ours should never be allowed to be abused.

We are mothers. We are not slaves.

Your Caretaking Legacy

This strike tactic may not be one you need to instate, but the policy of sharing the home duties most assuredly is. Even if your temperament is not one so bold (this same mother also sent her physician a bill for the additional two hours she sat in the waiting room of his office before he got around to her appointment), you should take your stand. If you think you are simply placed on this earth to mop up after your family, then why are you surprised that your family thinks that of you as well?

What counts is not that so many of the household duties are "below you," it's the family's attitude when you perform those duties. As you are teaching them to respect you, they will be learning a good work ethic that will serve them well all throughout life.

As Hamilton W. Mabie said, "A mother loves her child most divinely, not when she surrounds him with comfort and anticipates his wants, but when she resolutely holds him to the highest standards and is content with nothing less than his best."

What a mother *does* in life is so much more influential than what a mother *says*. If you speak with kind words, your daughter will. If carefully ponder what entertainment you enjoy, your daughter will.

If you treat others and yourself with kindness and respect, your daughter will.

If you develop your talents, she will develop hers.

Ultimately, when a girl leaves to begin her own life, the decisions she makes are hers. But what you demonstrate at home gives her the tools to formulate those decisions. It's not only the job choices or food choices you make that influence your daughter; your life and character choices will have the most significant impact.

Acting in the Best Interest of All

A story has been passed down through my family that is indeed true of my Grandmother Bunger. It was sometime in the rearing of her many children that she found herself battling for the financial care of her family. Upon receiving his pay from the railroad, my grandfather would stop by the local tavern on his way home after work. There the check would be cashed, drinking and gambling would finish out the evening, and he would arrive back at the family's door after drinking too much with less than livable money in his pocket.

Grandma had children to feed and a home to maintain. This was her priority. One day, after getting the kids off to school, this diminutive woman put on coat, hat, and gloves, then left her home. Walking first to the railroad station and into the office of the paymaster, she made her first defense for her family.

There, in no uncertain words, she told him she would be picking up her husband's check in the future. Adamantly she stated that she had many mouths to feed, and every red cent was needed to accomplish that task. Giving it directly to her husband would not be acceptable. She would see that the money made its way home, so she would be at his office to collect the paycheck at the end of the day that the checks were issued. While this could not be accomplished today without a court order, amazingly, this man agreed to her terms.

After that, she marched to the local tavern and gave that business owner a piece of her mind. Telling him that her husband was a father with many responsibilities, she let the owner know that this establishment was not an appropriate place for her husband to spend his money. If the story runs true, Grandma Bunger's visit got Grandpa banned from the building. So, he had no further opportunity to leave his family's welfare in that place.

It's interesting. My grandmother has never spoken of this tale herself. Her children and her children's children are the ones who passed it on to me. Grandma Bunger always took the high road. I never heard her speak of my grandfather or treat him with anything other than utmost respect, kindness, and love. He was her husband.

Grandma Bunger always took the high road.

But neither would she allow him to make decisions that would destroy their family. Her disposition was always to hold her own while treating everyone with grace; she would right wrong and, at the same time, offer mercy. Perhaps because early in life she was in need of those same traits, she valued them so highly. She was masterful at combining the strength of character with unconditional love.

It is not noble to let a husband destroy his family or his wife. As the wife, you are worthy of respect and gracious treatment from your husband, just as a husband should be treated in the same way by you. Verbal or physical abuse is not acceptable from a spouse—*either* spouse.

If as a mother you are accepting conduct from your husband that is destructive to you and your family, your example is flawed at best. Your acceptance will teach your daughter that compliance is necessary for peace. It is never peace that is earned in such situations. What always takes place is the shrinking of one human character—the mother. Whoever a mother was meant to be, whatever she was to accomplish would be minimized under the destructive acts of their spouse.

This then would be the Home Demonstration that your daughter would see and believe to be right. No amount of words said, no counseling given could ever have the same impact as the relationship displayed in front of your child.

It's not only how others treat you but how you treat others that will be your legacy to your daughters. If you want your daughter to become a generous and loving woman who cares for other people, then you need to be that generous and loving woman.

No amount of words said, no counseling given could ever have the same impact as the relationship lived in front of your child.

Go on a family mission trip. Support a child in another country. Help build a house. Volunteer at the food kitchen. Pack a Shoe Box at Christmas or take an angel from the tree in the mall to buy a child's gift. Look for the big things that have an impact and do them.

While incorporating those into your life are wonderful and right, are you that woman every day?

Make your daughter's friends feel welcome at your home. Love them, listen to them, hug them, and make them know how special they are. Open a door for a stranger. Let someone else get the parking spot closer to the door. Say a kind word to the harried clerk at the department store, even though you have waited in line for twenty very long minutes.

If we're not kind, can we expect our daughters to be? They will not be generous unless we have been. They will not seek and respond to the needs of others if we fail to. When a daughter sees her mother is caring, even (as we all are) imperfectly so, she will know that is what she wants to be as well.

Wonder why your daughter may bend the rules or not tell the "exact" truth? Indeed, life experience has taught me the reality of sin nature, but a more permanent influence comes from example. Integrity is becoming scarce in our society but holds so much importance. Short of life creating no alternative, it is a fundamental task to fulfill the terms of a contract, whether it's an employment agreement, a rental contract, a house purchase, or a bank loan. You don't cheat on your taxes or embezzle from your employer.

But it's just as important to never walk out of work with pens and paper that you are using for school supplies. It is imperative if given the incorrect change from a purchase, more than was due, that you immediately return it. And if you happen to make it all the way home with that change, you must drive back and turn it in (they will think you insane; but do it anyway). If someone drops $10 on the dressing room floor, you take it to customer service. You don't call in sick from work if you aren't ill. You don't lie, big or small.

Every day these things are observed by your daughter. Telling your daughter not to cheat on school work, pay what she owes, and keep her commitments when you haven't will gain you nothing but her deaf ear. Don't expect anything from her that you won't commit to yourself. Your demonstration on the home front will tell her exactly what you are willing to allow in your life as well as hers.

I have had the privilege of following in the footsteps of some of the finest women I have ever known. Ethel Anna Bunger, Alena Elizabeth Brock, Shirley Bill, and Minnie Ethel Brock are names of women none of you know, but they are women who made an indelible mark in my life—and in most everyone they encountered.

None of these women, now gone, left behind a sizeable financial inheritance. They did not have buildings named for them, nor did they lead great institutions. When they did leave this earth, they left it a better place. The wealth inherited from their lives was personal; everyone who knew them benefited by the richness of their character. It was a legacy of strength over adversity, joy with each day, commitment to truth and integrity, deeply founded faith, and unlimited love and grace for every person that entered their lives. Their character had both Grit and Grace. They were strong women whose history is left largely unrecorded, but their impact was made and will continue to endure in the generations after them.

Their feats were not noble. They were ordinary kindnesses, ordinary acts, and they lived ordinary lives. But these extraordinary women were profound in their effect. They were the finest of In-Home Demonstrators.

If we know what matters most is not what we say, but what we do, perhaps we will be the one leaving the footsteps that are proudly followed by the next generations. Maybe we can make it into someone else's list of "People Who Have Influenced Me Most."

But most of all, we'll be leaving a legacy that our daughters and their daughters will be blessed to follow. We too will be women of Grit and Grace.

13

MILITARY STRATEGIST

| JOB DESCRIPTION |

Plan the conduct of warfare. Plan and strategize campaigns, the movement, and disposition of forces, and the deception of the enemy.

"IT'S A GIRL!" The announcement was made in a small room— cold, sterile, unfamiliar, and filled with a group of people who were mostly strangers, people I had met all within the last twenty-four hours... well, nineteen hours to be exact. Each minute had been agonizing and relentless. But the end had arrived. The smiles behind their surgical masks showed in their eyes when the announcement came.

Next, there was a loud, resounding cry. To my relief, my baby was healthy.

Every emotion that has ever entered my heart cascaded like Niagara Falls at that moment. Relief, love, pride, uncertainty, weariness, joy, and fear gave way to anxiousness to see and hold my baby. My husband had walked over to where they were cleaning her little body off from the process of birth. I kept asking him questions, but he was too awestruck to answer to my satisfaction.

Then, finally, they brought her to me. She was beautiful! I was amazed at the miracle. Only days before she was a kick in the rib, a blur in the ultrasound, increasing weight on the scale, and a dream. Now she was my daughter. All I could do at that moment was to cry. I touched her face, her brand-new, delicate skin. Pulling her foot out from the blanket, I counted her toes. Her foot was so little, so perfect. It had an arch and toenails. As my forefinger met her hand, she wrapped her five tiny fingers around mine and looked me square in the eye. At that moment, my daughter owned my heart, my life, and my best. It was hers until I died.

The Best Defense

What I didn't know that day was I had entered into a war. I had joined the ranks of the soldier defending family and home, fighting for those they love. I had not gone to the recruitment office and signed any contract. I didn't even know when I became pregnant that I would find myself in battle. This revelation came later when I discovered my child had enemies who wanted to effect change in her heart, corrupt her mind, and destroy her. Every child does. They had their plan, and that plan was not for the well-being of my girl. This enemy's appearance sometimes seemed innocuous, with no discernable malicious purpose. At other times it was apparent they intended to inflict harm.

Some people genuinely believe they are right in what they want to share with your child, in what they want to teach. But they are not. They also can be oblivious to their destructive agenda. It is you, the mother, who needs to recognize those enemies.

This child was placed in your care with a strategic purpose. As her family, you should be the one place she will find safety, committed daily to her best. She has been entrusted to you and needs your best defense. You as the mother, are to be armed for warfare.

As in any conflict, there should be Rules of Engagement—rules for battle and conduct while at war. The military describes this as "a directive issued by a competent military authority that the limitations and circumstances under which forces will initiate and prosecute combat engagements with other forces encountered." Okay, a lawyer wrote that, but what it means is that there are rules about what a soldier should do when attacked and how he or she should fight back. This instruction is given before shipping off.

As a mother, you're not exactly shipping off, but you are venturing into uncharted territory. The territory you are entering is filled with enemies and landmines. An effective Military Strategist in the form of a mother should have her guidelines as she marches into war. These are just a few:

›   You are your daughter's ally as well as her defender. She must know that you love her unconditionally.

›   Be diligent, observant, and informed of the enemies to your daughter's well-being. Guard your daughter against those who want to attack and destroy.

›   Be prepared, armed, and equipped to mount an effective defense. No opportunity should be given for an enemy to gain ground in your child's mind and heart.

›   Identify allies in the battle and partner with them to increase strength against hostility.

›   Instruct and prepare your daughter to one day fight her own battles. It is your responsibility to make sure when you are no longer there to fight for her that she can defend herself.

›   Conduct all actions on behalf of your daughter with integrity, truth, and grace. You must treat all persons with dignity and respect even if they are taking enemy positions toward your daughter.

If you are worried about the war, rest assured that we as mothers are made for battle. Fighting is not all that difficult for us moms; it comes easy. We have infinite stamina when determined and purposed. By nature, we are more tuned into people's feelings than our male counterparts, giving us the ability to catch our daughter's emotions as well as those around them.

We are capable of seeing past the presentation of a person to observe the intent of a heart. Also, we possess an incredibly useful radar called *women's intuition*.

We are soldiers with great endurance. We outlast most around us on a daily basis; we keep battling. If nothing else, we probably could talk our enemy to death! It shouldn't be our weapon of choice, but our strength in the area of communication is a great example of our unstoppable nature.

While taking up a defense for our daughters, we must be sure we understand the war we are waging and the enemy in our battle. Information about the world our daughter lives in is crucial to an effective battle plan. A clueless mother is a dangerous one. You cannot battle something of which you are unaware. You must be informed. You must know what is being taught in your daughter's school, among her friends, in social media, within her culture. Without that knowledge and understanding, you won't be able to defend your daughter effectively. You'll be without the tools you need to arm yourself and then wage each battle.

A clueless mother is a dangerous one. You cannot battle something of which you are unaware.

Don't fool yourself that your daughter is not capable of being her own worst enemy. She is. Whether it is self-image, defiant nature, or aligning herself with circumstances or friends who bring her into dangerous territory, you have to guard her even against herself. Rules are a must to keep her from entering a place in life where she is vulnerable.

Always remember, though, that while guarding against her own mistakes, she must build up her defense weapons and armor. Overprotection is just as dangerous as under protection.

There are also allies, partners in this battle who will encourage you, support you, and instruct you. They'll help both you and your daughter. As in all wars, allies are essential to winning. So, find those people—become their ally and fight together. They can be among her teachers, her friends, a mentor, your friends, or even in the most unusual places. Don't overlook any potential partner; he or she is priceless. They will make you and your daughter stronger for the fight.

Learning from failure

Conflicts will sometimes be won and sometimes lost. Each of the victories will be sweet; every defeat will be agonizing. But when you lose, do not be discouraged! Take heart: many of the battles that seem so defeating bring the best results. Easy times and success do not teach the best life lessons. More often, the best lessons are learned in what is at first believed to be a failure.

Defeat instructs both you and your daughter how to get up and fight again, as well as what to do next time. Your daughter will make mistakes, and so will you. And that's fine. Learning through heartache is the best instruction available. Our goal is to avoid mistakes that may alter the course of life.

As a mother, we want so badly to prevent those decisions. The ones that result in an untimely pregnancy, an alliance with peers that brings physical or emotional destruction, an auto accident with life-changing results, or disease contracted because of a momentary lapse. There are so many life-altering possibilities for our daughters that even the thought of them can be paralyzing.

Know this: even if and when mistakes are made, life goes on. We will never stop loving our daughters through theirs and pick ourselves up when we make ours. It's what we do with our mistakes that builds character and makes us strong. Simply never give up. Know this: grace is ahead. No matter what action or decision you or your daughter made in the fight, grace, and mercy can be yours. Grace and mercy *will be* yours.

It is the willingness to go to war to create and act upon that military strategy that determines the successful mother in battle. Making motherhood a life priority and commitment to do your best is all that is truly needed for your daughter. Whether you spend your days on the home front or outside the home, your first role is to be a mother first. Cleaning the family bathroom or writing a legal document should never interfere with the battles you will be required to wage.

Grandma Moses

American culture has many treasures, and one of these is the legacy of Grandma Moses. The memories of this woman who lived to be 101 years old, spanning the turn of the nineteenth century, are enduring on canvas. Her artistic creations brought her fame after she was already eighty years of age. Mother of ten children, with only five who lived, a rural farmer's wife, widowed at sixty-seven, Grandma Moses was a fascinating piece of the fabric of our country.

When she became a painter in her seventies because her arthritis was too painful to continue her embroidery, she portrayed in her art the life that she knew. Rural pictures of American life hung in some of the most prestigious art galleries in the world. Her paintings were admired by the most powerful as well as the poorest. The simplicity in her creation, as well as the simplicity of her life, spoke volumes to many. And her enduring wisdom supersedes her craft. Stated in this quote stated late in life. *"Life is what we make it. Always has been; always will be."*

So, as mothers, why should we work so hard in this unrelenting battle? Why should we look for the enemies and create a strategy? Because the final result of our effort is crucial. You are helping to shape a human life—your daughter's. It is not the book we write, the car we help manufacture, the store we run, the letter we type, nor the house we clean that will affect the generations that follow. It is the daughters we bring into this world and help to mold. They are our treasures, and they will be this world's treasure as well.

In these simple lyrics of John Mayer, the family life and love cycle are profoundly portrayed.

> *"So, fathers, be good to your daughters*
> *Daughters will love like you do*
> *Girls become lovers who turn into mothers*
> *So, mothers be good to your daughters too."*

Military Strategist, plan and execute well. There is no more profound joy in life but to see your daughter become what she is destined to be—with the strength, grace, and courage to face her future, fulfill her destiny, and follow her dreams. The day she leaves your home to set out on her own, you will know it was worth the cost, the commitment, the fight.

Conclusion

TAKE THE JOB!

| JOB DESCRIPTION |

Seeking women willing to take one of the most important jobs in the world—raising great girls. A position you need to accept; no experience necessary. Perfection not required.

MY JOURNEY THAT began as a doctor visit turned into one of the most rewarding, frustrating, challenging, delightful, and agonizing of jobs I have ever undertaken. The unexpected results of that day became the job that has impacted my life the most. This undertaking has not only shaped the lives of my daughters but mine as well. I have gained strength, grace, resilience, patience, been given mercy, and learned how to give mercy. It has brought me greater rewards than any other endeavor I have known.

My two daughters are the treasure of my life, and I have no regrets...not because I did everything right, but because I wholeheartedly committed to this life mission performing it to the best of my ability.

The most important thing that I learned is this, to be a good mother, you simply have to accept the job. It is not the birth of a baby, the marriage that brought your girl, or the adoption papers signed, but the job itself. So, say yes. *Take this job!*

There have been countless women who have had children while never making a conscious decision that this would indeed be their life occupation. Instead, predetermine that you will be one when challenged to stand up. As long days turn into late nights, you stay on call. You mend injuries, dry tears, encourage and protect, staying attuned to the needs of your child. You are the one to expect their very best. The rules are yours to set, which you do, and to enforce, which you will. The range of emotion will plunge from delight to heartbreak and back to joy again, yet you will stay on course, determined to complete this task.

The love of a mother transcends logic; we will stand by our children even when others think we are foolish. We believe in them when their choices or actions may belie that we should. It is when we demonstrate that kind of love that we are a mere reflection of its purest form. The kind that my faith teaches me well, love as it's described in I Corinthians 13:4-8 (NLT)

"Love is patient and kind. Love is not jealous or boastful or proud or rude. It does not demand its own way. It is not irritable, and it keeps no record of being wronged. It does not rejoice about injustice but rejoices whenever the truth wins out. Love never gives up, never loses faith, is always hopeful, and endures through every circumstance."

Are we patient and kind, not all days, but can we try. Jealous of other mothers, boastful about our own parenting? We need each other so we shouldn't be either one. Do we demand our own way? We try not to if our priority is that of our family.

But I think the portion that embodies the role of a mother the most accurately is that we never give up. We never lose faith, we always hope and yes, we always endure. Most daughters will challenge you. Whether it comes in two-year-old defiance, through middle school pressure, in high school rebellion or your adult child's life choices, a daughter will test. Even when they do, a mother will love.

A mother will never lose faith in what her girl can be, even when the choices she makes are taking her off course. When she has compromised the principals, she once held, when she finds herself entrapped in addiction, a bad relationship or a compromised life. Not only will we love, but we will still know their potential, we will see the good in our child when their conduct speaks otherwise.

These times are when the testing of our job is at its peak. It is upon us to never lose hope and to always endure. We will remember that there is promise in every girl, in every situation. When others judge your daughter, you will not. Instead, you will love her; you will not apologize for her or defend her. You will stand by her.

You mom, know the treasures that lie within her, the tenderness in her heart, the joyful moments she can bring to life, the depth of her imagination, the talents and abilities she possesses. You will remember them, recognize they are still there today and encourage them for tomorrow. Because as the next verse in that text says, "Love never fails."

So. Mom, accept this job.

There is not a more fulfilling life career than being a mother. I can confidently assure you the rewards will forever be worth any amount of pain. You may have your own President, or maybe you are raising the mother of a President. Whatever your daughter's destiny you can help make it happen!

As fearful and overwhelming this may seem some days, I can assure you that this is worthwhile. These will be memories found in ordinary days that are priceless in their worth.

When you:

› Hold your two-year-old, and she twirls your hair entwined with hers, whispering, "I love you, Mommy."

› Arrive at the elementary school and, upon entering your daughter's classroom, she leaps from her desk, runs across the room, and throws her arms around your legs.

› The day the girl came into your life as a stepdaughter, foster child or through adoption finally knows you as Mom.

› Have a cackle of "middle-school" girls underfoot in the kitchen as you are trying to find something for the clan to eat, and they are regaling every minute detail of their overly dramatic lives.

› Become the one mother the high school group is okay with attending the extra-curricular event, even though they know you enforce the rules.

› Are asked to be the special person to help decorate your daughter's dorm room as she leaves home for her first real "independent" venture into life.

› Pick up the phone at all hours, day and night. Because you are the one she calls with grown-up questions about grown-up life.

› Stand by your daughter even in disappointment, being at times the only one who sees the best, believes the best and hopes for the best, although her life choices are not bringing the best.

Then you know taking the job was worth all you gave—including the tears, the frustration, and the sheer delights.

The effect of successful mothers has been lauded for centuries and is better said by others than me:

Let France have good mothers, and she will have good sons.

—NAPOLEON BONAPARTE

For the mother is and must be, whether she knows it or not, the greatest, strongest and most lasting teacher her children have.

—HANNAH W. SMITH

Who is it that loves me and will love me forever with an affection which no chance, no misery, no crime of mine can do away? It is you, my mother.

—THOMAS CARLYLE

One of the oldest human needs is having someone to wonder
where you are when you don't come home at night.

—MARGARET MEAD

The mother is the most precious possessions of the nation,
so precious that society advances its highest well-being
when it protects the functions of the mother.

—ELLEN KEY

All that I am and hope to be I owe to my angel mother.

—ABRAHAM LINCOLN

These statements and many others like them are only said when speaking of Mom. Accolades made from the platform of an awards presentation or a family at the dining room table declares the worth of a good mother. The impact this position can make is undisputed.

So now you know. At least you know a lot of the jobs that need to be done. It may look a lot more like work to you than the day you found out you were going to gain the title "mom" or even when you began this book. But don't let that scare you. This really is an achievable as well as delightful job and you are the one who can do it. Every one of our daughters desperately *needs* for you to take this job.

Mom, take the job. You can do this; it is not an impossible task. In fact, the rewards are great. You'll be building a remarkable relationship with a fantastic girl...*your girl.* Together you and she will learn, grow, accomplish, and conquer things you never thought possible.

Know that your girl will have the opportunity to excel in life—to become everything she is created to be. Just because you, her mom, commit to take and complete one of the most important jobs in the world: raising great girls.

For the dads

A JOB FOR DADS!

| JOB DESCRIPTION |

Embrace and exhibit the best characteristics of a man's nature and set the guidelines for acceptable behavior. As the first man in a daughter's life, create the standard for all who follow.

THE DAY WE discovered we were expecting a child my husband was perfectly calm. Like most of the male gender, he is the steady one who virtually never becomes unnerved, unlike his female counterpart, which would be me. So, when we discovered we were having a baby, his reaction, while excited, was slow and steady. Other than the realization that his responsibility had increased significantly, he appeared unfazed that our life would be turned on its head with this new little person.

I, on the other hand, expressed immediate terror that we were going to have a child. But the day that I discovered our child was going to be a girl, my anxiety rose to a whole new level. Maybe it is because I, being the female, had slightly more understanding of the challenges that were coming.

Perhaps it was the seemingly non-stop morning sickness, or pure exhaustion that tipped the balance. Whatever the cause, my anxiety elevated beyond rational thought.

In hindsight, I believe that I did understand my gender, but I was also the parent who would create entire plays in my head illustrating every future event with hypothetically terrifying consequences. I would find myself imagining our daughter's life choices with pitfalls and problems that wouldn't have a happy ending. Without his steady life outlook, I would have probably been more of a blithering idiot than I already was.

His trepidation about raising his daughters did come. It was quite a few years after we brought her home from the hospital. The arrival of his unnerving landed when our first daughter entered the preteen stage. This season she was in full swing of how a preteen female can act. I saw my steady, always calm, never flustered husband look at me with complete bewilderment. There was this "Who is this girl, and where has my daughter gone?" look of panic on his face.

What had transpired was the sweet little princess that had crawled up on daddy's lap since she could crawl had launched into an illogical, emotional storm that only she understood. From screeching fury to unexplainable crying the emotional whirlwind ended with the "you just don't understand." Our little girl completed her twenty-minute performance stomping up the steps then slammed the door to her bedroom. This was not daddy's little girl (if you haven't gotten here yet dads, don't let this derail you, this phase does pass). This was one of the evil witches that were prominent in the Disney films he had been forced to watch with her. And he possessed not one bit of understanding of how to handle it.

It was during these years, the ones he could not comprehend what had transpired or who this girl had become, that he doubted his impact on her life. I told him as I will tell all dads from the day they are born through their entire life, girls need their daddy. Even when everything in your girl adamantly states she doesn't want you near her or need anything you have to offer, she does.

Here's why. While either parent is capable of doing all parenting jobs, there are some that are better performed by the mom, and there are most certainly jobs much more effective when fulfilled by the dad. Your woman can bring you up to speed on the mom jobs earlier in this book (many of which you will share with her).

But, I want to take just a little bit of your time and let you know what the jobs that, to create the most impact, are yours. Also, I will give you a few examples of how to do it, as well as share a few insights from dads who performed these jobs well.

This will not be too long or be laborious reading because if you're anything like my husband you want a lot of life in "Cliffs Notes." I understand that you're busy and unlike most females, you don't need all of the details.

Let me encourage you with this, there are days I wonder where all the dads have gone, but if you're reading this, you aren't one of them. So, kudos to you for caring enough to take the time to gain a little more insight on what it takes to do this job we call dad.

1

MASTER GEMOLOGIST

| JOB DESCRIPTION |

A Gemologist possesses the ability to establish the quality and value of gemstones assessing their clarity grading and using their identification skills to determine their worth. Understanding the market factors that will influence their final value.

Y OU MAY BE wondering when a woman wants to share something she deems significant, does she have to begin the conversation with gemstones and jewelry? I just can't help it! A Master Gemologist is a job every dad needs to take. It's the most important position you need to grasp, then perform, when raising your daughter.

There are primary functions of a Master Gemologist, which are applicable for the job of dad. The most important is that you realize that you are the first, as well as the most influential individual, to determine the value of the gems you assess (in this case is your little girl). You are also in the unique position to assess the "market factors" that will influence your daughter's perceived value by others. Then it is yours to prepare her to assess these factors for herself.

Deciphering "market factors" is not to say a father intends that his daughter grows up to be considered a commodity. It is quite the opposite. It is taking the information you have gleaned from the culture she will be entering, then applying that understanding for her benefit. When this job is done well, she will believe that she indeed is a treasure of great worth. You will be the first male to help her realize how valuable she is, unwilling to be esteemed any less. You will also be the most effective.

It does not matter if you are the hunting, fishing, kind of guy going to work each day in blue jeans and work boots, or the businessman who wears a suit and tie spending his days at an executive desk. This job can be done well no matter what you do, or what you wear. It's performed well by who you are.

Here's the secret to the dad version of a Gemologist. If you take the time to let her know she is priceless and worthy of respect, love, and admiration she will believe she is. If you don't take that time, she will forever wonder what her value may be. Then another male who does not have your little girl's interest at heart will one day set the value for her. Does this terrify you dad? It probably should, so be there first.

As you may have already discovered (because of your involvement with this girls' mother), we females can be confusing. Some days we act like we need a man in our lives, while other times, we act as if we can do it all on our own. But the reality is this. Females seek the attention and approval of men whether our gender wants to admit it or not! This is true of your little girl as well.

It is your job to value this treasure, your daughter, before any other man does.

I can guarantee that if you love your little girl well, she will have a much better chance of seeking the love of a good man. She won't be found looking for love and attention from the wrong men. I can promise you Dad; the day will come and seek she will.

How to do that is pretty simple. When you talk about gems you speak of clarity, flaws, cut. A Master Gemologist is the one to quantify the worth of the gem by recognizing its unique qualities and preparing it for the market. Dad, you are the one to quantify the value of your daughter, treasuring her unique attributes and getting her ready to face the "market" she will enter.

Let's take a typical day. You may have worked with difficult tasks or demanding people all day long. Perhaps you have expended an enormous amount of physical labor. Maybe you are the company leader and are exhausted from the human demands placed upon you. You arrive home from that hard day to find your little girl in her princess outfit awaiting you on the doorstep.

She immediately drags you into the house to plant you in a chair and chatter incessantly about the silly things little princesses chatter about. After completing your exhausting day, the only thing you want to do is turn on the TV, check the news online, or take a shower. The one thing you do not want to do is sit still for this miniature royalty. But indeed, at least occasionally, you must.

A friend of mine recently discovered this reality then posted about his enlightened moment on my author page on Facebook. I know him as a road manager, sound engineer, one-time member of a SWAT team and guard in a security services company. He's a man's man, not necessarily the-hanging-with-princess type. I find this story enlightening, a complete departure from the adventuresome, rough and tumble kind of guy that he is.

Ok, the past month has been crazy, my wife flying all over the earth (private jet pilot for the well to do) while I've been the SAHD (stay at home daddy). Last night I lay on my youngest daughter's bed while she colored and talked, and talked and talked, for a long time getting the day off her chest. I was surprised what went on in a four-year-olds head. After quite a prolonged period, she looked at me and said, "Daddy, you let me talk a very long time." She turned and then got out of her little chair. Coming to where I was laying she placed her four-year-old head on my chest and said, "Thank you, daddy." I had a "wow" moment.

Last night was something. I mean I'm a good daddy, but it was like this veil was taken back. EVERYTHING I do and say, are the things that give my daughters the good and bad. How I react to momma when I'm mad shows them how a man treats a woman. I get to determine the mindset of the man she wants...it's all very frightening...and awesome...man....my daughter's think men should all carry guns, tell SWAT stories and cry at family movies......

He's really on the right path with this one. There's a practical side to the Dad Gemologist. That is making your daughter feel valuable from a very young age.

I want you to stay with me here Dads before we go on I need to give you the "why" for doing this. The day will come when your little girl will venture out on her own. Most begin their quest for independence in middle school with the desire to choose friends you may not know. Then comes High School which brings more decisions that she will want to make for herself, venturing into new places, building new relationships and exploring new opportunities. These years are the beginning of the outside influences that will impact her perceived value.

Her final step toward building her own life will come as she packs up her belongings to leave home, in the pursuit of a degree or to advance her chosen career. As she ventures into each of these new areas of independence, there will be influencers who often challenge her value. She may have friends whose fickle loyalty quickly extends to the most exciting new person in their lives; leaving her wondering why that isn't her. She will most likely experience education challenges, boyfriend drama, and career disappointment.

Each of these things can shake the self-worth and self-confidence of any daughter, even those who learned their worth early in life. But for those girls who have not heard they were precious in value, it may not merely shake their self-worth, but it has the potential to destroy it. Performing this job well, early in your daughter's life is providing her a life jacket she can grab ahold of before she even knew she needed one.

I have to give you guys a break here when it comes to female chatter. Listening to every word we females say can be incredibly time consuming and tiresome. Yes, we use three times the number of words you do to complete the same thought. Yes, we can talk about an array of subjects, both interesting and mundane.

Remember it isn't every word your daughter says every day that you must listen to. It's that you need to set aside specific time to listen with total attention allowing no interruption. Not a whole lot different than the adult female in your life. We don't need all of your attention all of the time. We just need undivided attentiveness that is entirely ours, without distraction, some of the time.

It's not just listening to your daughter, but it's talking to her as well. She needs to hear what you think of her. Does she make you smile and laugh? Tell her. Does she amaze you with some of the things she does? Tell her. Are you proud of one of her accomplishments? Tell her. Do you think she looks pretty? Tell her. The individual moments that take just a very few seconds add up to an exponential increase in how your little girl values herself. She will believe what you say; you're her Daddy. And by the way, if you ever wonder, the grownup female in your life isn't a lot different!

What I don't want you to do is to tell that little girl she's great when she's not doing what she should, when her conduct is defiance or disobedience (she will do that as well). Trust me, she will see right through that. If you always tell her she's great no matter what she does, it leads her to believe she can manipulate the male species. I'm sure you've met grownup women who have mastered that talent. It's not very pretty, so you don't want that easily-acquired ability fostered in your daughter.

Know that there will be times when your daughter will act in ways and make choices that will frustrate and even anger you. This conduct can come in the form of five-year-old disobedience or later as teen rebellion. Even though you may be disappointed in her choices, she needs to know you will always stand by her and never quit loving her. Your love should be constant, and your love should be unconditional. By being the one who loves no matter what, you are showing her the kind of love you want her to one day receive from another.

She will believe what you say; you're her Daddy.

There's one more thing a Master Gemologist Dad should do that's slightly different than simply dealing with a gemstone. Being a man, you intimately understand the "marketplace of life" and need to educate your daughter so she can understand it as well. While it is true that your actions will speak the loudest, there are some things said by a dad, that a girl will dismiss from her mother.

You need to take any opportunity you have to help her see what an excellent "buyer" looks like. No, you are not putting your daughter on the market. You are helping her to fully understand how others will or will not place value on her by giving her the insights needed to recognize those who will appreciate what you do—her great worth.

Tell her what you expect from any young man that wants to be in her life. She may sigh, roll her eyes and say "Oh, daddy" but every qualification you give she will hear. Whether on the day that you share the information or later when she is serious about some young man your words will resonate in her heart.

There is a desire in every little girl that is treasured by her father; she will want him to approve of the man she will one day come to love. She does not want to disappoint her dad. You may not believe that to be true, but I promise you it is. Let her know what kind of guy that needs to be, and she will never forget. Tell her repeatedly and begin when she is young.

Here is a simple list of suggestions, words your daughter needs to hear from her daddy:

› *He should possess common courtesy. If he says, he's going to call your daughter let her know he should. If he says, he will arrive at a particular time make sure she understands short of an auto accident or family emergency; he must. His integrity in the little things is an accurate indicator of his integrity in the big things. Your girl should know this.*

› *He must be willing and able to look you in the eye and answer any question asked without hesitation. Your daughter needs to understand that you expect this.*

› *He must have a work ethic. Whether in sports, job, or education he must believe that he has to work for anything good in life and be willing to do that. Your daughter must understand it takes hard work for anything worthwhile, including a healthy relationship.*

› *His "love" should be shown not in what he wants but in what he's willing to give. Unfortunately, our culture teaches that "love" means your little girl surrenders herself emotionally and physically to whoever makes the statement of love in a relationship. Help her realize that unselfishness is the real definition of the word love. A guy can love a pizza, devour it, then leave the table and move on to something new. True love by a young man means he will treasure her, not consume her. She is not made to be merely the physical gratification of another. She is worth so much more than that.*

I know you may have many more expectations than just those four. Determine the standards that you want to express to your girl, ones that are important to *you*. Add them, reiterate them and make sure your daughter grasps them.

The final thing you need to help your little girl understand, one terrifying to most parents, is that the young man she may one day end up with will impact the rest of her life. Today's statistics don't guarantee that a young woman will find a man deserving of her commitment. Another reason a girl needs to believe in her self-worth.

But if she does pursue this relationship, you want to make sure she knows what the right one looks like. The young man she chooses to leave her parents for will hopefully encourage her to be even more than who he married because he treasures her. She will do the same for him.

Their lives will be intertwined; they will share everything. So, the final assessment will be this—are they compatible in the real world? Do they share values, have cohesive views on finances, share their faith, value integrity, and have they considered children? If you have set the bar, having taught that such critical topics of conversations between genders are something to be pursued, she will be comfortable engaging in the same conversations with the man she hopes to share her life.

So, here's a recap, Master Gemologist. Make sure your daughter treasures herself in the same way you do. Listen well. Encourage much. Love unconditionally. Explain the marketplace of life.

And remember this, how you treat the women in your life, the grown one and the one you call daughter, will be how she believes a man treats a woman.

If you do this job well, embedded in your little girl's heart will be an understanding that she is one of your great life's treasure. This truth will make her stronger, braver and successful in all that she accomplishes because you made her believe she was priceless.

2

STUNT COORDINATOR

| JOB DESCRIPTION |

A Stunt Coordinator must have experience as a former stunt person, one who is daring, creative and risk-taking by nature; can troubleshoot and is attentive to safety. Must have the capacity to pay close attention to details and think quickly.

ANYONE WHO HAS traveled the rural roads in the American South has seen at least one barn roof painted with the words "See Rock City" a tourist destination atop Lookout Mountain in Chattanooga, Tennessee. The mountain is aptly named because when moving through the Rock City acres you come upon several precipices comprised of ledges barely large enough to stand, giving you the opportunity to experience a view of seven states. We visited that particular park when our younger daughter was one and our elder daughter five.

As we wound our way along "The Enchanted Trail" we approached an incredibly narrow rock platform suspended over a 100-foot drop with a fantastic view. A railing comprised of three horizontal metal bars broken vertically about every four feet, enclosed this ledge. My husband holding the one-year-old in one arm took the five-year-old by the hand and walked to the very edge of the barrier. He then proceeded to lean over the railing to tell them about the seven states they were viewing.

At that moment, the only thing I could see was that my one-year-old was suspended mid-air past the intended barrier. Not only that, my five-year-old was sticking her body through the said railing attached to her daddy only by her skinny little arm. As all sane mothers do, I shrieked to my sweet husband, "Are you kidding me? BACK AWAY FROM THERE WITH THOSE GIRLS!!!!" He looked at me as if I had fireworks shooting out of my head, which wasn't that far off. Then quietly stated, "They're fine. They wanted to see the view."

When my husband realized that I was on the verge of a complete meltdown, embarrassing to the entire family, he graciously stepped back for my sanity's sake. The fear of my daughters plunging to their deaths soon subsided. Feeling a bit foolish I apologized. I also explained *at length*, as all females do, the reason for my outburst as we continued toward the completion of our Rock City experience. The truth is our daughters never were in real danger. He had them. He is their daddy.

There is something through the years I have come to understand about my husband's risk-taking relationship with our daughters. In a real-life way, he was actively teaching them life possibilities.

I am not a fearful female when it comes to my safety. There are very few risks I'm not willing to take. But when my daughters are involved, I default to protective "momma bear" (as most mothers do). It was he, being willing to let them reach past the ledge, who helped them love adventure, believing they could accomplish things that other people would tell them were too difficult or dangerous. He was their Stunt Coordinator.

As stated in the job description, Stunt Coordinators have already accomplished the stunt. Their experience in life risks makes them uniquely qualified to coordinate the risk of those with which they work. They are creative, risk takers, with an acute awareness of safety and attention to fine details. They also determine the time and place the stunt needs to occur.

As a male, you are by nature more daring and a greater risk taker than your female counterpart, especially when it comes to your children. Yes, that is completely politically incorrect. But even if I were to be politically correct, this statement would still be true. You are the one who can quantify the risk, manage your daughter's safety and determine when the stunt needs to take place. Being a risk taker is a great thing, and it's a great thing to instill in your daughter.

Our first daughter, like normal two-year-olds, had particular people she delighted in seeing. One of those was a dear friend, a member of one of the rock bands that we managed. Part of my work in those years was promoting concerts in several U.S. states. When I did, I would take her on the tour bus with me. She would start her morning by jumping out of the bunks, barrel through the stage door and across the stage to plant herself in front of this particular musician she was crazy about.

She stood there quietly waiting for the question she knew he would ask, "Loren, would you like for me to you to hold you, upside down by one leg?" She would vigorously nod her head while excitedly repeating the word "yes!". His next step was to grab one leg, turning her upon her head and dangle her upside down. This act included walking around backstage over cords, equipment and other stage gear showing her the theater from this skewed vantage point.

She would giggle until she could hardly breathe, then before she turned blue and fainted he would set her upright and just walk away to do his job. She loved those moments and jumped for the opportunity with abandonment. This was a simple act, but at two she was already learning that he could be trusted to guard against the potential risk of her landing on her head. Because of that, it was a risk she was more than willing to take.

You are, by nature more daring and a greater risk taker than your female counterpart.

A Stunt Coordinator, well, coordinates. That seems like such a silly sentence. Although he often does the stunts himself, part of his job is to encourage those he is working with that no matter the task ahead it is achievable for them. When it comes to your daughter, it is not just teaching physical risks. It is taking risks in opportunity as well.

I think it's worth telling the story of another father, who in unlikely times and unusual circumstances helped his daughter achieve great things. Before I share this story, I must add that in my telling there is no condoning of slavery. This story only serves to display that within a vastly flawed culture a father's impact on his daughter's life not only changes her trajectory, but it can also help to improve the lives of those around her.

It was 1738, a time well before a business opportunity was afforded to women, in the midst of tensions increasing between Britain and Spain, Lieutenant Colonel George Lucas moved his family to South Carolina where he believed they would be safe. The Lucas' father had acquired three tracts of land that held a total of 5,100 acres, property that would create an entirely new product in the South.

Shortly after the family's move, the Lt. Col. was called back to the West Indies, where he served the British Military as the Lieutenant Governor of the island. For safety reasons, he left his wife and children behind.

It was soon after his departure that his wife Ann died, leaving 17-year-old Eliza as head of the family and overseer of their land. Lt. Col. Lucas did not doubt Eliza's ability to rise to the occasion, so he handed the leadership into the capable hands of this young lady. She was later recorded saying, "I have the business of 3 plantations to transact which requires much writing and more business and fatigue of other sorts than you can imagine, but lest you should imagine it too burdensome to a girl at my early time of life give me leave to assure you I think myself happy.[14]"

As an educated girl which is something her father insisted upon, she had mastered the writings of Milton, and John Locke and fluently spoke French. But unlike other plantation owners, she chose to display her unique nature by sharing her education with unlikely students, the children of the plantation slaves.

It was her love of learning botany that brought success to the crops of South Carolina. Eliza's interest in the potential of the land she oversaw held no bounds, and neither did the high expectations of her father.

Lucas encouraged his daughter to further her sights by exploring different potential crops that could create a new industry in the fields they were planting. Upon her request, he shipped indigo seeds: the plant used to make indigo dye, grown only in France or the West Indies at the time. Drawing upon the unlikely assistance of the knowledgeable plantation slaves, Eliza sought insights from the very ones who understood the land they worked. Together they began the challenging work of cultivating and developing a new strain that would grow in the soil of the South Carolina foothills.

After one season's disappointing failure, the tenacious Eliza wrote to her father, "I am sorry we lost this season. We can do nothing towards it now but make the works ready for next year." It was through the combined determination of Eliza, her father's belief, and the assistance and abilities of those who worked the land that they finally accomplished their goal three years later. This marked the beginning of a new industry.

The reason I think this story is relevant is that Lt. Col. Lucas believed in this daughter and encouraged her to take the helm. She took a risk on a crop that had never been grown outside of France and the West Indies and introduced it to America. Even in the midst of apparent failure, this father stuck by his young, single daughter encouraging her to stay the course. He believed in her and helped her believe in herself, thus becoming willing to take the risk. By doing so, an industry was launched, and a young woman discovered within herself the great things of which she was capable.

There is another reason this role of Stunt Coordinator is so right for every dad; it has to do with our gender's nature. Fear is an easy emotion for females. We often worry more, are more introspective, more protective, and on our most fearful days, it can lead us to stop ourselves from doing something before we even start. Something as simple as a local news story affects us a bit differently than it does your gender—rendering more fear.

Because we want our daughters to live full and productive lives, it is your job as the father to counter every one of the fears she may hold. To do this, you have to understand your daughter's temperament. You may have one girl that is a risk taker caring not at all about damage done, while the other doesn't want to get too dirty in the process. My husband had both. So, you adjust your risk-taking for their temperament in the same way a Stunt Coordinate tailors the stunts to the person performing them.

An effective Stunt Coordinator for daughters also does a great job of explaining and exposing their daughter to risks. This builds in each little girl the confidence that they can accomplish much with minimal fear. Find the physical activities that suit both you and your daughter. It will be different for every dad and daughter. Consider the options—sports, hunting, rock climbing, trailblazing, shooting, white water rapids, biking, motorcycle riding.

Both of our daughters rode on the back of their dad's Harley from the time they were little. We bought a child-sized helmet, gave them instructions on the proper way to ride, then placed them behind their daddy to pull out of the driveway for their adventure. We didn't have to teach them to hold on tight; they did that automatically. I knew their dad would do everything to make sure they were safe as I sent them off, but that didn't stop this mom from immediately calling out to God to send angels along each side of that motorcycle. The girls loved it, and as grown young women both are looking forward to a day they can afford to purchase their own motorcycles.

By teaching risk, you are also teaching independence. Your daughter's reality is this—finding a man worth marrying and then actually having a successful marriage is not a slam dunk by any means. It is necessary in the world today that your girl can live as an independent woman. You want that little girl to grow up able to take care of herself. There is no guarantee that every daughter will find that good man to share life with. She may even have landed with a man that's not so great, then finds herself alone again.

Having the ability to fend for herself involves education followed by career opportunity and career risks. Challenge them to pursue the education that is necessary to obtain a job that is meant for their unique talents and abilities. Be willing to encourage them that whatever they take on within their gifts they can accomplish.

Assist them in finding schools that offer what they need to gain the training required for their career path. Then, Dad, you have to do the hardest part. Encourage them to leave your home, perhaps even your community to obtain that education. Support them as they take the risk to pursue their chosen career. As much as most fathers want to shelter their little girls the day will come when you have to allow them to take the risks they must take all by themselves.

You've prepared them for it, you've taught them to be brave, to believe in themselves, and to do things they never thought they could. When they fall, they have learned how to get back up again. You have been a capable Stunt Coordinator teaching them to be willing to do their own stunts with the confidence that they will master them. When the day comes for them to walk out the door and pursue their purpose, you know you've done your job. They will be ready. Ready to face whatever comes their way.

-3-

BODYGUARD

| JOB DESCRIPTION |

A Bodyguard must be able to protect the client by any means necessary, ensuring safety in his or her home. Scope perimeter of all locations prior to arrival assessing threats, establishing all entrances and exits. Possess the ability to balance the protection of the client with their need and desire to live a normal life. Qualified to continually monitor potential threats, educate the client to vulnerabilities and create an exit strategy should one become necessary.

Now that you have successfully taught the value of taking life risks, you would be completing only part of your role if you were not to take this next job. This position requires that you protect your daughter from and then teach her about life's danger. You may remember the intense plotline of the film *Taken* that clutched the hearts of many parents, including me. From the terror of that first phone call to the pursuit of her captors, it was easy to relate to Liam Neeson's character. This father, at whatever the cost, was going to find his daughter who had been abducted and return her home. I believe most fathers would do the same.

While the overall percentage of children who are abducted by non-family members is relatively small, girls comprise 74% of those taken. We also face the fact that one out of every six women in America is a victim of attempted or successful sexual attacks.

I am going to fly in the face of many of my gender with this next statement—protecting the females in your life is an honorable and much needed, task for a man to do. I am not insinuating that my gender is weak. We are not. Anyone who tries to cross a woman, dead set on whatever mission she has decided to undertake understands the falsehood of that assumption. It is a dangerous place to land between a woman and where she's determined to go. What I am saying, however, is that females have vulnerabilities that men do not.

So, Dad not only do you have to be a masterful Stunt Coordinator. You also have to provide the services of a Bodyguard as well, protecting your daughter. Then you will be tasked to teach her how to protect herself. This is a job for which I know you are well-suited.

A successful Bodyguard will draw from an established set of principles. I do realize that in recent years there have been some highly questionable antics by some members of the Secret Service. Even with some who don't seem to uphold these principals, I find that their statement of core values is a perfect foundation for anyone taking this badge of commitment to protecting another:

> Each point of the Secret Service star represents one of the agency's five core values: justice, duty, courage, honesty, and loyalty. These values, and the Secret Service motto "Worthy of Trust and Confidence," resonate with each man and woman who has sworn the oath to uphold them across the agency.[15]

I believe every female feels safe with a man who embodies these values. A father who personifies these tenets will not only fulfill this job of protecting his daughter; he will also be a real-life example of the type of man she should one day put her faith in, a man "Worthy of Trust and Confidence."

The first duty as you become your daughter's Bodyguard is to ensure safety on the home front. A father's presence in a daughter's life is paramount to her feeling safe.

As a little girl, I often awakened fearing the product of my imagination—a monster of nondescript proportions that I was sure, resided underneath my bed. It would paralyze me. I would move myself to the absolute center so that no matter how long the monster's arm was, he could not reach me. I was also sure if I cried out, he would jump from under the bed and attack. It was in those hours of my unrealistic fears that my only comfort was my dad's snoring. When I heard it, I knew that all was well. It wasn't that he was the Navy Seal type. Chasing bad guys wasn't in his wheelhouse. He was an accountant with a day job that entailed running a calculator. But I felt safe because I knew he was there.

Life conditions or obligations may not allow you to be ever-present. Your work may require frequent travel or demand long hours. Your daughter may live with her mother which creates separation for more extended periods of time. But understand this. Physical presence is important, much more vital is a father's emotional presence. Some fathers reside in the same home yet are never really there.

When your daughter knows she is your priority, she will feel protected. When she understands that you will stand with her and by her in all circumstances, even when you are disappointed in her or confused by her, she will feel safe. This is as simple as knowing her Bodyguard is within calling distance. Even if that protector is standing guard outside of the home and had to set a security system they set in place, they can rest well.

Physical presence is important, much more vital is a father's emotional presence.

There is another duty in the job of Bodyguard—understanding the world your daughter is living in. You must scope out the locations at which she will arrive and the individuals in attendance to remove threats. Let me tell you a story that will explain this concept better.

We have a dear friend who has successfully performed the job of Bodyguard in raising his two daughters. This was on display the year his younger daughter went to her Senior Prom. We were staying at their home the same weekend of this auspicious event and participated in the evening. Three couples were attending Prom together and on limited budgets. So, the plan was to have dinner served for said couples, at our friend's home then send them off to their final Prom.

Their daughter spent the afternoon readying herself for her special evening, boyfriend arriving right on time to be her escort. Each of the other four landed on their doorstep dressed and ready for that evening meal. We ushered the couples into the dining room, the table set with good china, glassware and appropriate silverware. Then we proceeded to serve them attending to their every need as if they were at a restaurant, giving them room to chat and just be teenagers. Completely ignoring the parental type servers, these six teens had a great time. It was at the conclusion of the meal that the attitude of servitude no longer extended, and parental authority stepped back in. This change in disposition was directed to the boys in the group.

What took place next is fondly entitled "The Precious Cargo Talk." Before these young men's food had the chance to digest they were led into this father's study. With obvious discomfort on each of their three faces, they were going to hear what the night's expectation would be. The father's conversation went something like this:

"You are leaving my home with precious cargo. Each of these young ladies, who are your dates, are extremely valuable and should be treated as such. If you wonder what that means I will explain."

"There will be no drugs. There will be no drinking. You will go straight to the prom, and you will deliver your date home on time as agreed to, not a minute late."

"There will be absolutely no sex. That means any kind of sex. Unlike what you may have heard oral sex is still sex. There will not even be any hands placed in inappropriate places. And let me be clear what inappropriate means. Below the neck to above the knees of each of these precious girls is off limits."

"They are the treasure of every one of their parents, and you will be expected to treat them as such. If you don't, you will reckon with me, and I promise you it will not be pleasant. Now have a good time."

You really should have seen their faces when they came out. They were ashen! These trembling boys had been warned. I almost felt sorry for them until I watched as the three teenage girls in their pretty dresses followed their dates into the limo. For the rest of the evening, they would be well out of the view of parental supervision. My sympathy was short-lived. This was a priceless Father Bodyguard moment!

Whether it is the lure of a stranger, a bullying classmate, driving a car, or going to the prom, every father should protect his little girl by scoping out all the risks facing his daughter every day.

The third responsibility is to teach them to recognize potential threats. They must acquire self-defense should they need it and be prepared with an exit strategy to avoid hurt or harm.

It is in the pre-to-early elementary age that we begin teaching them to recognize these threats. The first lesson is to be cautious of strangers. Without instilling unnecessary fear or extinguishing your little girl's ability to recognize healthy interaction, this is a conversation that you must have.

There is a tip I have found invaluable that I have shared with moms earlier in this book regarding this subject. There is a simple policy you can create then discuss as a family to safeguard your daughter from the strangers whose intention is harm. Agree upon a secret word, one to be used if this occasion should arise.

This word is only known to those within your inner circle. You will choose, as a family, what that word will be. Make sure it's something that holds no logic in the stranger scenario. This can be a favorite food, a special animal, even a made-up word that your daughter creates (as long as everyone can remember it). Just make sure your daughter knows if she is approached by anyone she doesn't know, she asks one question, "What is my secret word?" If they can't answer that; it doesn't matter what they tell her, she will know you did not send them.

Another threat that a Bodyguard needs to thoroughly assess is the world of the Internet. In the same way, you would physically stand between your daughter and an individual who might harm her, you need to stand between her and the information, conversations or attacks that can come in social media as well as through Internet exploration.

The first time your daughter crosses the street, it is not by herself. Neither should she be venturing alone as she enters the world of the Internet. This is an area where it is vital that the Bodyguard job includes scoping the perimeter, assessing the threats and establishing the exits. You must possess the understanding of what dangers exist, then take steps to safeguard the device she is using from venturing places you do not want her to go.

In her first few entries navigating this world browse the internet with her. Make this a benign activity, assisting her as she finds things of interest that you would approve of. There are some great online games, funny videos and learning activities to explore. You might even venture into the girly stuff that makes no sense to you whatsoever, but she delights in. Just make sure she knows where she's allowed to venture, and where she is not, as well as the present dangers. As she begins her early foray into this arena, you would be wise to enable parental controls on all your devices, creating one more layer of protection.

As she grows older, her continued navigation into this technology becomes increasingly mobile and takes place away from the home front. It will take an artful observation, protection, and trust to be a successful Bodyguard in this ever-changing world. There are programs you can subscribe to that help you monitor while protecting her privacy. You will find there will be seasons you restrain activity and seasons you give freedom. These decisions will be based on the age, maturity and proven responsibility of your daughter. But I think the best protection as she grows is continuing to encourage her to make good personal choices and cling to behavior that will keep her safe in every area of her life.

Make sure she knows where she's allowed
to venture, and where she is not,
as well as the present dangers.

There is one area every girl will face that a father understands all too well—the time they begin their interaction with boys. Whether you like it or not, they will enter her life. It may be a good idea to begin this particular instruction by taking your daughter on her first date when she's still a little girl. This will give you the opportunity to set the standard. You will be demonstrating how the boy who lands on your doorstep for your daughter's first "real" date should act. Or you could just follow the example of one dad who made this statement when boys arrived at his home with the intention of leaving with his daughter, "Yes, my daughter is beautiful, but I have a gun, a shovel, and an alibi."

While that may not be your best introductory statement, you do know these boys. You've been one. There is not a thing wrong with having the same conversation with *your daughter* as my friend had with his daughter's Prom date. It will probably seem to be one of the most uncomfortable discussions a father can have, but that's what makes it so much more effective.

A mother knows how a female thinks simply because that is her gender. An explanation of how your gender thinks, feels and reacts coming from a male is so much more believable. Remind yourself as you take on this duty of a Bodyguard that there is only one reason you would put yourself in this position—that is to protect her. You may want to take a dry run with the lady in your life just to make sure you can pull this off. Gaining a little practice before the big show may help. But, as uncomfortable as this discussion may be, it is well worth the effort.

The last duty is often a difficult one for dads. You must find the balance between protecting your little girl and allowing her to live a healthy, risk-taking life. The most challenging season of that part of the job will be her teen years. But Dads, I will start here. If you've been the Bodyguard for the years before she hits her teens, teaching her to recognize a threat and defend against it, she is prepared.

Whether your instruction has included the establishment of policy, warning against predators or even a self-defense class or two ending with exit strategies, your final goal is this: protect your daughter until she can protect herself. You want her to have the understanding/wisdom/common sense as well as the emotional and physical skill sets required to do so.

Part of that instruction happens while she is still under your roof by allowing her to experience life a little at a time on her way to independence. Let's take driving for instance. After getting her driver's license, and demanding her freedom, start small. Maybe first send her to the grocery by herself. What parent doesn't need a few errands off their plate?

Then allow her to only drive to school with one friend in the car. After that nighttime driving with that same one friend. Next, she will be loading her group into the car as they make their way to their high school's sports event, a movie, or a concert. This will soon follow with the request to take the car on a day trip, which later becomes an overnight event.

These are natural progressions you have to allow in the season your daughter has proven herself able to handle them, with your instructions and exit strategy intact. Seatbelts on every person in the vehicle, no drinking or drugs, and the destination must be the one that was presented.

It was March of her senior year that our that elder daughter asked if she could drive herself and four friends on a four-hour road trip to visit a nearby college. They would spend the night and return the next morning. Realizing that a mere five months from this request she would be literally thousands of miles away as a college freshman, we felt we had to say "yes." But this "yes" came with a discussion that went something like this.

"You are to be the only driver, and you will do so with caution, staying within the speed limit, and minimizing all distractions. Should a tragic accident occur in which the lives of your friends be altered forever or even lost, it is not only the grief that will be excruciating. We will likely be sued and lose our home, our business, your college tuition, and our family's future. So, taking care in this trip is paramount to our approval of you going."

The terror on her face was priceless, and I believe at that moment she wondered if she really wanted to go. We wanted her to understand the most extreme case scenario, but one we have seen played out in others' lives. We left the decision up to her. The good news was, she did head out of town on that trip with a car full, arriving safely home the next evening.

As you work toward allowing your daughter more freedom with the goal of independence, your final instruction should always be this, "I will trust you until the day you prove to me you are not worthy of my trust. When that happens, it will be a long and arduous road to regain it." This is your safeguard for this is part of the job, balancing protection with the need and desire to live a normal life.

When you choose to accept this last job of Bodyguard, protecting and conducting yourself in the best interest of your daughter, you will find success. Note that I said *success*. Not perfection. Not without failure or setbacks. But success in the long-term, achieving your ultimate goal, rearing a daughter who realizes she is a talented and self-confident individual who strides into her future making her impact on the path she has chosen. When she ventures from your home to tackle the world, she will enter it prepared because after you have protected her, you have taught her how to confidently protect herself.

Dads

TAKE THE JOB!
IT'S A POSITION YOU'LL NEVER REGRET.

| JOB DESCRIPTION |

A dad wants to catch you before you fall but instead picks you up after you do, brushes you off and lets you try again. He wants to keep you from making mistakes but loves you enough to allow you to find your way even though his heart breaks when you get hurt. He will hold you when you cry, scold you when you break the rules, shine with pride when you succeed, and have faith in you even when you fail.

S o, now you have it. There are jobs a dad is well suited for, and when you do them, they will make a world of difference in the future of that little girl who has entered your life. These positions you can accomplish will help that her become, while imperfect, an amazingly strong young woman. One who can discern what is bad, good or great life choices, then has the nerve to pursue the great ones. She will do this because you believed she could and made her believe it too. Even when she doesn't choose the great ones, she will know her value will never change in the heart of her father.

Performing this job well does not require a degree, a study or a personality type; she may be your little girl biologically, through marriage or adoption. You may want to take her fishing, and she might want to drag you to *Disney on Ice*. She may be a soccer star, and your only interest was music.

Daddy-daughter combinations come in all variations. You just need to know that it doesn't matter what your interests are, what job you hold or what style of clothing you wear, you are the right daddy for the little girl placed into your life. It is a perfect combination that does not require perfection.

Music serves to be a backdrop to much of our lives, and it's in the lyrics of a song written by Ben Folds for his daughter, Gracie, that I believe speaks well to the incredible love of a father for his little girl.

Gracie
You can't-fool me; I saw you when you came out
You got your momma's taste, but you got my mouth
And you will always have a part of me
Nobody else is ever going to see
Gracie girl

With your cards to your chest walking on your toes
What you got in the box only Gracie knows
And I would never try to make you be
Anything you didn't really want to be
Gracie girl

Life flies by in seconds
You're not a baby Gracie; you're my friend
You'll be a lady soon but until then
You gotta do what I say

You nodded off in my arms watching TV
I won't move you an inch even though my arm's asleep

One day you're gonna want to go
I hope we taught you everything you need to know
Gracie girl

And there will always be a part of me
Nobody else is ever gonna see but you and me
My little girl
My Gracie girl[16]

So, Dad, it's your job, too. Your woman shouldn't have to do it on her own. She needs you to partner with her for this significant undertaking. Yes, you will be there to share in all the jobs, but even more to exhibit the traits that are displayed and performed the best by you.

When you see your little girl leave your home to pursue her dreams as the strong, confident, talented young woman you always knew she would be, you will know it was worth all you gave. As you watch her forge a life of accomplishment, as a girl who is rich in character, you will be glad you took this job, the job called Dad.

About The Author

Darlene Brock. Co-Founder and President of The Grit and Grace Project, Author, and Co-Host of This Grit and Grace Life Podcast left home at 18. Her first pay your rent job was a receptionist at a prestigious law firm, which she left to live in a Christian commune. As her life pendulum swung again, she took the job of running a summer camp and conference center before spending the next 20 plus years in the music business. One to always enjoy a new adventure, Darlene once para-glided off the Bavarian Alps with her two daughters; you just can't put this lady in a box.

It was not long after leaving home at that young age; she realized embracing grit and grace were the traits that got her through many trials and triumphs. It was this realization that led her to launch her most recent venture, The Grit and Grace Project with co-founder and husband, Dan.

In addition to the podcast, "This Grit and Grace Life," this organization currently produce a women's online lifestyle magazine. Every element of The Grit and Grace Project, including their book publishing affiliate, was created to remind women that true beauty is found in a woman's strength.

As Darlene embraced grit and grace to master the challenges in her life, she became inspired to write about raising confident and capable daughters, understanding that perfection was not required. Holding to the belief that a woman's self-confidence and strength is best gained at a young age it was her goal to arm mothers with the tools they need to complete the job of raising great (but not perfect) girls.

Having two adult daughters, she understands that motherhood is not just one job, but it is many. To set any girl in your charge on a life course for potential success requires mastering a broad range of positions. In different seasons of a girl's life. From Coach to Military Strategist, every mother takes on various responsibilities when embracing the title of mom.

Darlene has been featured on the Fox & Friends morning show, Focus on the Family and Family Life Today radio programs, and multiple ABC, CBS, NBC and FOX affiliates. She has been a featured columnist for CNN and written for numerous Family oriented magazines and websites.

It was in the busyness of producing award-winning music videos, managing music groups, promoting concerts and serving as COO of ForeFront Records that Darlene raised her two daughters. This unique blend of author, mother, businesswoman, wife, and creative producer has shown her that it is indeed true, "life challenges should neither defeat nor define you." And just so you know, she wears the tool belt in her family.

The Grit and Grace Project

The Grit and Grace Project was co-founded in 2011 by Darlene Brock with business partner and husband, Dan R. Brock. The company, established to publish books, e-books, and other materials, was created to inspire women to discover their inherent strength.

In 2015 a separate company, under the same name, was launched as a 501c3 non-profit corporation. With this debut as a women's online lifestyle magazine, thegritandgraceproject.org provides insights, how-to's and tips on real beauty, relationships, work, finances, motherhood, purpose, and faith. The articles are written by real women who have discovered within themselves the grit and grace needed to conquer the challenges of a woman's life. Every insight delivered in such a way that women feel encouraged and inspired, often laughing along the way.

The next unveiling of The Grit and Grace Project was in Fall of 2017, producing This Grit and Grace Life Podcast, co-hosted by Darlene and Julie Graham. This cross-generational weekly podcast is like having a cup of coffee with your best friends, being part of the conversation as these ladies tackle hot-topics and issues facing all women, with occasional visits from great guests who will join to talk about some of the more difficult subjects. From the boardroom to the bedroom, car-lines to college, single married or single again you'll leave each episode with women's tips and advice on all things life.

No matter what the undertaking The Grit and Grace Project entities have done or will do, all driven by the belief that true beauty is found in a woman's strength.

For more information go to thegritandgraceproject.org.

Endnotes

1. https://nces.ed.gov/programs/digest/d15/tables/dt15_318.30. asp?current=yes
2. https://www.nawbo.org/resources/women-business-owner-statistics
3. 19 June, 2003; http://news.bbc.co.uk/2/hi/uk_news/3002946.stm
4. https://www.psychologytoday.com/articles/200307/ the-new-sex-scorecard
5. http://www.cam.ac.uk/research/news/ males-and-females-differ-in-specific-brain-structures
6. https://www.cdc.gov/healthyyouth/sexualbehaviors/
7. https://www.kff.org/other/ kaiser-family-foundation-seventeen-surveys/
8. http://depressivedisorder.blogspot.com/2013/01/early-sex-teens-causes-depression-suicide.html
9. http://www.acpeds.org/the-college-speaks/position-statements/ gender-ideology-harms-children
10. http://www.moron.nl/lyrics.php?id=36043&artist=Big%20 Bad%20Voodoo%20Daddy, accessed December 14, 2010.
11. https://studentaid.ed.gov/sa/about/data-center/student/portfolio
12. https://lendedu.com/news/race-gender-paying-for-college/
13. https://www.psychologytoday.com/articles/200901/ marked-mayhem
14. From letterbook of Eliza Luca, afterwards Mrs Charles Pickney, 1739-1762 Pickney Family Papers, South Carolina Historical Society, Charleston.
15. http://www.secretservice.gov/FY2008_AnnualReport_WM.pdf
16. Songwriters: Benjamin Scott Folds © Warner/Chappell Music, Inc., BMG Rights Management US, LLC Scripture quotations are taken from the HOLY BIBLE, NEW INTERNATIONAL VERSION·. niv·. Copyright © 1973, 1978, 1984 by Biblica, Inc™. Used by permission. All rights reserved worldwide.